You Will Never Get It Right By Doing It

Wrong!

20 *Success-Crushing* Mistakes
You Didn't Know You Were Making

Bill Quain, Ph.D.

You Will Never Get It Right By Doing It Wrong

20 *Success-Crushing* Mistakes You Didn't Know You Were Making

By Bill Quain, Ph.D.

ISBN: 978-0-9976132-0-9

Cover Design and Layout by Parry Design Studio, Inc.
www.parrydesign.com

ACKNOWLEDGEMENTS

As always, there is no way I could produce this book without the help of my team members:

Editor – Jeannine Norris

Layout, Design, Graphics, etc. – Jack and Elizabeth Parry, Parry Design Studio (www.parrydesign.com)

Book promotions/sales/distribution – Katherine Glover

Proof Reader/Listen-to-every-idea-no-matter-how-late-it-is (If you are married, or in a serious relationship, you know who I am about to thank) – my wife of nearly 32 years, Jeanne

DEDICATION

This book is dedicated to my father, William J. Quain, Sr.. Dad passed away while I was writing this book. He was a fantastic father, and I miss him every day.

When Dad was alive, he was always saying (about himself), "You're a lucky man Bill Quain." It was a phrase my mother used to say to him whenever he got a phone call from one of his children, or when we went fishing together, or any one of a thousand things that parents and children do.

At Dad's funeral last August, the theme of his eulogy was just that—"You're a lucky man Bill Quain."

Well, you know what Dad? You were a lucky man Bill Quain.

And so am I!

Thanks to you Dad, and to my family, friends and readers, for all the luck I have.

CONTENTS

A Special Note From The Author

Hi folks, it's Bill Quain. You are about to read one of the best books that I ever wrote. It is one of the best because it can really help you. But, before you start reading it, please read this short section carefully.

**Please do not read this book all at once.
This book is called a "random access book"
and should be read in a unique way.**

Read the Introduction and Chapter One, and then take a little break. Later, look at the Table of Contents and find a "Mistake" that looks intriguing, and *just read that one chapter!* Think about what you are reading, and then make a few notes for yourself. In a few days, choose another Mistake or two (anywhere in the book) and read. Remember: only one or two each time. Reflect on what you learned.

That's the way to read this book. Slowly.

WHY?

This isn't an ordinary book. It doesn't start at Chapter One, and then slowly build an argument or a message through the other chapters. You won't learn something small at first, and then get more information about the concept. It isn't a story that grows throughout the book.

No, this book has *twenty* chapters, each with a single, stand-alone mistake. You need some time with each one.

This book is meant to be a lasting guide for your life. If you take your time, give some serious thought to each of the mistakes I talk about, and then actually *do something about them*, you will be more successful, have better relationships, be more confident, and you will attract successful people to you when you start to make significant changes in your life.

But, if you just sit down and read this book, you are going to get too much information all at once. Your mind will jump from subject to subject.

Okay, that's it. That's all I wanted to say to you before you start reading this book. I *wrote* it for you. Now, you need to *read* it for you and your family.

INTRODUCTION
Mistakes? What Mistakes?

This book is all about mistakes. These are the mistakes that almost none of us know we are making. We make them every day. We are losing money, sleep, friendships, love, and our *futures* because we are making these mistakes.

In this book, I am going to talk about 20 of the most common mistakes you are making. How do I know that you are making these mistakes? Simple. We are all making these mistakes! We have been taught to make them. Our society, our schools, and our social systems all keep telling us to make them.

But, these well-meaning folks aren't saying "_____ (your name here), go out and make these mistakes." Society isn't telling you to do something bad. Your teachers and politicians aren't saying, "It is time to make the mistakes. Let's get ready, get set, go!"

If they were saying that, we would all catch on and STOP making these mistakes. But, that isn't the case. It isn't as simple as all that.

Instead, society (you know, all the people who spend time telling us what is the right thing to do) is saying to us, "Just keep on doing what you have always been doing. You are a good person. You know how to be a good citizen. Just do MORE of what you have been doing, and you will be successful."

You see, that's the real problem. The real problem is that you are making all these mistakes, and everyone is telling you that they are not mistakes. Everyone is saying, "You just need to do more." They tell you:

1. Do more work.
2. Save more money.
3. Stop thinking about the things you can't have.

4. Get a good education and listen to your teachers and professors.
5. Don't rock the boat.
6. Etc.

Your big problem isn't that you are making mistakes. Your big problem is that you have no idea that you are making these mistakes.

Let's Think About This

You are a reasonably intelligent person, right? I mean, you are reading this book, aren't you? This means that you have some intelligence. You can read a book like this and think about the things in this book. That is a reasonably intelligent thing to do.

Now, as a reasonably intelligent person, if you *knew* you were making a mistake, would you stop making it? Of course you would.

Now, what if you found out that you were making *20 mistakes*, maybe every day of your life. Would you, as a reasonably intelligent person stop making them? Of course.

So, What Can We Conclude From This?

If you are reasonably intelligent, and a reasonably intelligent person would stop making huge mistakes as soon as they realized what was going on, then we must conclude that you do not know that you are making mistakes! And, I am also going to make another leap here. I am going to tell you this:

You don't know that you are making these mistakes, because our society keeps telling you that you are doing everything right, and that you just need to do more of what you are already doing, and then you will be successful.

Folks, That's A Problem

We continue to hear, "Just work more and keep doing what you are doing. In the end, you will have everything you want. It is all going to work out. In the end, you will be able to retire successfully (after forty to fifty years of working hard—very hard). You will be fine if you do what you are doing, for a little longer, and with a little more energy."

Am I Getting Through?

Folks, this is the most dangerous thing you have ever faced. Not only are you making these crazy, self-destructive, dream-stealing mistakes, you think you are doing the right thing and so you do more of the same thing. In other words, you are convinced that you are not making mistakes, and you try to do more of the same thing—which is making mistakes!

Wow, I am Exhausted

I am going to ask you a simple question:

"How is it going for you?"

If you say to me, "Fabulous. I am doing just great. I have plenty of time and money. I am not stressed out. My kids are going to college and they do not have massive student debt. My financial future is secure, and I will have the time and money to enjoy my life."

Well then… I guess I would say that you are NOT making mistakes. You are doing the right things. Keep it up.

But folks, if you CAN'T say that, you are stressed out, and working too hard, and your financial future isn't secure, then just STOP. You are making mistakes, and making them more often, or for the next twenty years, isn't going to make your life better.

That's all I wanted to tell you in this introduction to the book. It is time to figure out what you are doing wrong, and stop it. Then, it is time to start doing the right things, and do *those things* for the rest of your life.

It isn't hard. It is a bit scary. It is a bit nerve-wracking to realize that the life you were leading (thinking you were doing the right things) is actually a mistake. That's a tough thing to learn.

But, it is the first step in turning it all around. It is the right thing to do.

Start With Mistake #1 And Then Choose Your Favorite

I want you to start with the first mistake: *Accepting Failure Instead Of Selling It As Experience.*

Folks, I just know this one is going to shock you to the bone. It is EXACTLY the opposite of what we have been taught.

Start there. It is the mistake that I learned about that got me to write this book. I want you to have the same shocking realization that I did.

After that, start choosing mistake titles at random. Look for the ones that intrigue you the most.

Finally, talk about these mistakes with your friends and colleagues. Talk about them with your spouse. Talk about them with smart, open-minded people. And when you do, resolve to stop making the biggest mistake of all—believing that you have not been making mistakes.

Enjoy!

MISTAKE

1

Accepting Failure
Instead of Selling it
As Experience

Okay, this one is really going to surprise you. About five years ago, I was at a meeting for business professors in Philadelphia. We had a luncheon speaker who was an angel investor. An angel investor is someone who lends money to start-up companies. He told us an incredible story. In fact, when I heard this story, it gave me the idea for this book. You see, he talked about an *incredible mistake* that business owners often make.

Here is his story:

His investment company lent $50 MILLION dollars to a tech start-up. I forget what kind of software, the tech company was supposed to develop, but it didn't go well, and in about six months, the tech company had burned through the $50 MILLION. That's right—6 months and $50 MILLION gone!

What did the executives from the tech company do? They came back to the investors and asked for $50 MILLION more! Can you believe it? Isn't that an amazing story? These guys had run right through the investment. The money was gone, and yet they had the courage to ask for another $50 MILLION.

What was the reason they gave? What possible rationale could they come up with to get the new money? Well, here is where I sat up and took notice, because like I just said, it is the whole reason behind this book.

The tech company executives said the following to the investors: "We need another $50 MILLION to get this software off the ground. You see, we made some mistakes as we tried to develop this software." ("No kidding!" was my first thought when I heard this story.) "But, *we learned* from those mistakes. We won't make them again, because it was an expensive lesson, and we will remember it. So, (and this is where it really got me) if you invest with us again, you will actually SAVE yourself money. If you invest your next $50 MILLION with someone else, they still need to make those mistakes!"

And so, the speaker told us, his company made another $50 MILLION investment—with the same people who just lost the first $50 MILLION.

What Would You Have Done If You Were The Tech Company's CEO?

This is a worthwhile question to ask yourself. Most of us would have skipped town, changed our names, hidden out of shame, and the vast majority of us would have thought, "I am such a failure. NOBODY will ever trust me again. I am so embarrassed that I can never show my face around here again."

Isn't that about right? Isn't that what most people would think?

But, real winners NEVER feel that failure is an obstacle to future success. In fact, real winners believe, in their very hearts and souls, that winning is directly related to looking forward, not backwards. You see, the real winners in this game of business are convinced that failure and mistakes are just part of the growing process. They say, "Okay, we made a mistake. So what? Let's get going again."

And why are these business winners able to do this? It is because they are focused on success. They aren't focused on the mistakes they made. Instead, they are saying, "Wow, I learned a lot. Think of how much faster I am going to succeed now."

Are You Focused On The Past, Or On Your Goals?

What about you? Where is your focus? If you invest in a business, and you lose some money in the first three months, are you the kind of person who slinks away, embarrassed about the failure? Or, are you the kind of person who says, "Well, I may have made some mistakes, but *my dream hasn't changed. My desire to succeed hasn't changed. The only thing that has changed is that I learned from my mistakes. Now, I am better equipped to succeed.*"

Why Are You So Embarrassed By Failure And Mistakes?

It's difficult to be the only one in your circle of family and friends who has a dream or goal that is different than everyone else. There are in-laws, spouses, friends, and acquaintances that are happy to say to you, "You see, that didn't work. Why didn't you listen to me? I tried to tell you that this would fail. What a terrible mistake you made."

It's hard to keep your focus when you have people like that who are waiting to say, "I told you so." I know it is. But those people aren't part of your success. Remember, those people have been making the same mistakes year after year. The difference between them and you is that they don't know they are making mistakes. They think they are doing the right thing—all the time.

You Are Already On A Different Level

Hey, you are reading this book for one purpose alone: to give yourself additional information and some additional *belief in yourself and your business.* Do you realize that already puts you on a different level than most people you know today? How many of them are taking the time to set goals and then do something about it? How many of them are trying something different—something new—in order to succeed? The answer is that probably very few of them are doing anything different. Instead, they get up every day and do the same things. The best that they can hope for is to be average, because they are doing the same things that every other average person is doing. They fear mistakes and failure, not because it will slow them down on the way to their dream, but because they don't want to be embarrassed.

That's not your level. You aren't afraid of the mistakes that you will make as you build your fortune. Instead, you are afraid of making the same mistakes that everyone else is making—and will continue to make.

Be Aware, But Don't Be Afraid or Ashamed

Okay, this step is easy. Just accept the fact that failure is a part of success. If you are trying to switch your thinking from a lifetime of working for someone else, in order to build a wonderful future for you and your family, did you think that you would get it right the first time? And, if you didn't get it right—if you made some mistakes— were you afraid that your reputation would be ruined? Okay, well that is the mistake! Your mistake wasn't losing some money. Your mistake wasn't talking to the wrong people. Your mistake was thinking that those things mattered. They don't.

Do You Get What I Am Saying Here? Do You See the Difference? I Just Have To Say It One More Time To Be Sure:

Your mistake wasn't losing money. Your mistake wasn't approaching the wrong market segment. Your mistake wasn't even the fact that you didn't know how to handle people properly. Your mistake was that you thought those things mattered. And, you thought they mattered because all the average people around you were telling you that they might matter. That was your mistake—believing them.

Decision Time

This book is all about becoming aware of the mistakes you are actively making, and then making a decision to do something about each one of them. This chapter is no different. What can you do about changing the way you think about your past failures? You can do two things. First, begin hanging around with successful people who have not let past mistakes hold them back. That's easy to do. Here's a hint: if someone gave you this book, or suggested that you should read it, then she/he is one of the people you should be hanging around with! Stop letting people steal your dreams.

The second thing you need to do is to keep your dream in front of you all the time. Focus on the present and the future—and let the past go. Do something positive every day, something that moves you forward. Did you make some big mistakes in the past? Okay, so did I. But now, don't turn those past mistakes into a fatal mistake.

I know you can do it.

MISTAKE

2 Being In Control Instead Of Being In Demand

If you are serious about making a breakout from the mediocre bonds that hold most average people in a near poverty level, then you need to read about this mistake twice—no, make that three times!

Okay, get yourself buckled in. I get pretty excited about this mistake. In fact, I may go on a bit of a rant!

I mentioned in the introduction to this book that "average people" are trying not to make mistakes. They go to school, maybe go to college, get some degrees and credentials, maybe even some certifications. They do all these things so that they can become successful—or at least successful as defined by the average people in our society. They are desperately trying to do the right thing all the time. And, as I hope you are beginning to realize, this is a huge mistake.

But what are these people really doing? They are trying to gain some control in their lives. They are controlling their destinies by sticking to a commonly held set of beliefs: get an education, work hard, don't cause trouble, and you will be fine. These people are always in control. They control their tempers, their children, their speed while driving, their work environment, and sadly, their imaginations. They also control their dreams. Why? They control their dreams in order to keep their dreams at a certain level. In other words, they don't want to have a big, wild, exciting dream. They want to have a controlled dream—one that they can attain if they spend their lives in total control.

Unfortunately, They Are NOT The Ones In Control

You see, in an effort to be in control, what they're really doing is turning over control of their lives to someone else. For example, they turn over control of their work lives to their bosses. After all, in almost every employer-employee relationship, it isn't the employee who is in control. The boss sets the hours of work, the work to be done, the pay scale, and the periodic raises and promotions. Not much control there for the employee!

The average person also turns over control of his/her life in other ways: elected officials, the police, the IRS, etc. Yes, in a democratic country we can vote for government officials, but does anybody really believe that the government is run democratically? Is there anyone alive today who really believes that the money paid out by special interest groups isn't the real power behind our elected officials—and therefore, the real power behind all of our laws and regulations?

In an effort to gain control, the average person spends a lifetime giving it up to others. And that's too bad. A lot of these average people have the ability, desires, and energy to take back control of their lives. I mean real control.

But What About "Demand?"

In the title to this chapter, I say that the mistake that is being made is trying to establish "control instead of demand." So, what do most people—the average people—think about demand? They are against it! They think *demand* is something bad, not something good. Consider this: when I use the word *demand*, I am talking about a powerful force that drives money, recognition and opportunity into people's lives. To my mind, demand is great. If you (or your services, advice, products, or company) are in demand, it means that people want what you have. It means that they will PAY for what you have. In fact, the higher the demand, the more they will pay. Demand is wonderful.

But, how do average people look at demand? What do they think demand is?

The average person—the one who is seeking control over his/her life—thinks of demand in quite a different way than truly successful people think of it. For example, you will hear average people say things like:

1. I have so many demands on my time. I can't stand it!

2. Everyone is demanding my attention, all day long. My boss, my spouse, and the kids, people I work with – *everyone wants my attention, and they all want it at the same time.*

3. I have so many demands on my life. Everyone wants me to volunteer for something or to sit on a committee. I have no balance in my life because of all the demands.

Can you see how average people perceive *demand* as a negative force? All of the *demands* that other people put on them means that they are running out of time, patience, money, etc. When their boss runs into the office and says, "We need this report done right away. Everyone should drop what they are doing and work on this. By the way, we are all going to stay here tonight until it is done." THAT is a negative demand.

But, what if *demands* were something positive? What if every new demand resulted in more money, more time, and less stress? Would that be different?

Supply and Demand

Everyone has heard the economists say things like, "It is a matter of supply and demand," right? In other words, if you are *supplying* something, then demand is just what you want. In fact, the more people demand something, the more valuable it becomes.

If you want to stop worrying about *control*, and start rejoicing in *demand* then you need to supply something that people want, and you need to have some way of supplying it so that it doesn't take up so much of your time.

An Example of Positive Demand

Suppose you want to make some significant changes in your life, and you know that those changes will require you to make more money. You can simply work more hours, but that is going to make "demand" a negative factor for you. You are going to have to give up time in order to meet the demand. This limits the amount of demand you can fulfill.

But, there is something you can do. For example, if you hear other people say, "I am feeling so tired in the afternoon. I wish there was some way for me to get through the day without being exhausted." Do you know what this is? It is *demand*! People have a demand for a product or service that will make them feel more energetic. But, they don't want to feel more energetic just because they want to feel more energetic. They want more energy so they can enjoy life more. They want to get their work done more quickly, or to be able to be more alert when they get home and spend time with their kids at night. *That is what they are demanding.*

What can make them feel more energetic? Several things come to mind: energy drinks, vitamins, exercise, weight loss, supplements, etc. All of these things can make a person feel more energetic, right?

But how does this affect you? Simple. What if you found a solution to their problem? What if you found a company that already had a product or service that would make all these people feel more energetic? And, what if you found some way to *make money*—simply by putting this company and those people together?

Old Control Versus New Demand

You see folks, the old way of thinking, keeping tight control, will kill the new way of thinking: finding demand and filling it. In the old, "control thinking" way, you would have to make the product, deliver it, collect money, distribute the products, etc. In the new way of thinking, you give up some of the control (all the things previously mentioned) and simply enjoy the benefits of bringing supply and demand together.

You introduce yourself to the supply company, and then you introduce the company to the people who are demanding the energy! (Let the company's website do the work, while you simply get a small piece of every transaction.)

I Want More Demand!

Folks, if you are getting a *reward* every time someone has a *demand*, do you know what you want? You want more demand, right? Suddenly, you are freeing yourself from that old way of thinking and learning to let go and enjoy the ride.

This is why I say that seeking control, instead of creating demand, is such a huge mistake. And, it is a mistake that is most often made by people who are trying to avoid making mistakes! (Ironic, isn't tit?)

Go ahead and lose a little control. In fact, *demand* it of yourself. All *you* need to do is to find a need and fill it—but do it in such a way that everyone else does the hard work!

MISTAKE

3

Choosing An Arrow Instead Of Choosing A Target

"What's this about arrows and targets?" You might question this a bit. "Why would you choose a target instead of the arrow?"

Here's a mistake that a lot of people make. They walk around with a quiver full of arrows, just looking for some kind of target. Are these real arrows? No, of course not. These are *metaphorical* arrows. In other words, over your lifetime you pick up a lot of arrows along the way. Everyone has different arrows: education, experience, skills and abilities, training—these are all arrows.

Many people's arrows are based on the things they like to do. For example, if someone likes to work with their hands, they may take a real interest in carpentry. Or, if someone is good in math, they may take a real interest in the sciences. People tend to build their quiver of arrows around their interests.

So here we all are, walking along life's path, with a quiver of arrows on our back. We have these tools and we are looking for a place to shoot them.

Is This Really A Problem? Isn't This What Everyone Else Does?

Actually, this is a big problem. As we grow up, we get separated into groups. We tend to hang out with people who like what we like. If you are an average smart person, are you likely to choose friends that are really, really bright? If you go to college, what kind of people are you attracted to? During our lifetimes, we find people who like us and who are like us. They are doing the same thing. Pretty soon, we are separated or segregated into groups and we spend a lifetime there.

We learn the same things and we believe the same things. We share our interests and we have a lot of arrows in common.

Let's take two college students as an example. The students both come from families who have a lot of college graduates in them. So, there is pressure in high school to become "college ready." Both of these students take academic courses, rather than courses like "shop" class. They learn to study and give teachers what they want and expect. They improve their writing and reading skills, and study college-level mathematics. These are all arrows that they put into their quivers.

But in college, they begin to separate into two different groups. One student (let's call her Helen) wants to help people. She decides to go into nursing. She learns how to take care of patients, work with doctors, fill out medical records, etc. She is a good student and she likes what she is studying. Along the way, she discovers that nurses make a nice living—but not nearly as nice as some other professions. But, it is too late. Her quiver is full of healthcare arrows.

On the other hand, Robert decides to study marketing. He learns a lot of marketing theory from his professors. His quiver of arrows is full of things like team building, accounting, management techniques, etc. With his quiver of arrows, he can probably make more money in his job than Helen can. But, he has been taught a certain kind of marketing and business management. His professors are traditional instructors. They are teaching the students how to get a job in a big corporation.

As both of these students graduate and progress through life, have families, and build careers, they tend to look at every problem through the "eyes of their arrows." For example, when Helen and her husband decide that they need more money in order to send their kids to a good school, Helen reaches over her shoulder and grabs her healthcare arrows. What does she do to get more money? She picks up extra shifts at a nursing home on the weekends.

Robert and his wife find themselves in the same position. They need some more money in order to maintain the lifestyle that they want. How does Robert go about getting more money? He reaches back in his quiver of arrows and finds his business arrows there. He has learned negotiating skills, so he pulls out that arrow and shoots it at his boss. (Well, remember this is not a real arrow!) Robert goes to his boss to try to negotiate a higher salary.

On The Average, Arrows Work Just Fine

Both Robert and Helen are great examples of how average people try to achieve average goals. They take their arrows, the things that they already know and believe, and try to apply them to average targets. The problem is, the only targets that they can see are the same targets that all the other average people see. These are the "I'm going to work hard so I don't get fired" targets. Or maybe the "I want to have a nice second car" target. All this is great if you are happy with average targets.

Can You See The Mistake Coming?

Here is the mistake: when you concentrate on the arrows, you will never see new targets. However, if you concentrate on the target first, you will not be limited in your choices. For example, many average people say things like "people like us can never have *that*", so they don't even try to achieve extraordinary things. Or, they might see someone that they know, someone who has a lot of time and money and freedom, and think to themselves "Well, with my quiver of arrows, I will never be able to have that. I better aim at a target I can hit."

Can you see how concentrating on your arrows limits your choice of targets? Are you beginning to understand that this is a mistake that almost everyone makes? At this point, I want to help you become aware of this mistake.

What Happens When You Choose An Exciting Target?

Let's face it folks, arrows are never exciting. Arrows are just the tools we use to get what we want. Yet, modern society has convinced us that it is the *arrows* that we should be working towards: get a masters degree, learn a great trade, or improve computer skills. These are the kinds of things we are encouraged to do. But, what if we changed all that? *What if we started talking about the targets instead of the arrows?*

This could change everything, couldn't it? Let's look at our college students again to see how this might work.

Helen loves healthcare because she loves helping other people. But while she's in school, she runs across some people who are going to teach her how to think big. They say to Helen, "How would you like to make a lot of money so that you could help people?" In other words, they start showing Helen a different target. They start talking about targets with really huge impacts on the lives and wellbeing of others. Suddenly, instead of thinking about learning how to be a nurse, Helen starts thinking about how to use her skills, experiences, training, education, and her passions in such a way that she creates sustainable, powerful healthcare systems for others. And, she starts dreaming about how to do this in such a way that she still has time to raise a family. Suddenly, Helen's target turns into something really big. She starts thinking about how to attain huge goals, while at the same time balancing her life so that her children will get lots of attention. She now has a different target.

But, how can Helen achieve that target? After all, she has been trained as a nurse. Well, what kind of arrows does she have in her quiver? She still has the basic skill sets that a nurse has. She has learned a little bit about medicine and taking care of others. But now, she suddenly finds herself needing some new arrows. She is going to have to learn something about business. For example, maybe Helen decides to sell nutritional products to people. Instead of looking for sick people to help, she is now looking for healthy people to help—she wants to help keep them healthy. She creates a business and begins to build with some new arrows in her quiver.

Robert finds himself in the same situation. His plan was to get a good job, work hard, get periodic raises, and make a great salary. He knew he was going to trade a lot of time for dollars in order to do this. But one day, he meets a man who is an entrepreneur. This man owns his own company. He works for himself. Soon, Robert has a new target. He doesn't want just a good job, he wants the rewards of business: money, choices, prestige, etc. He starts thinking about what he learned in college (his arrows) and realizes he needs some new knowledge (more arrows) in order to hit his target.

Instead of relying on his old textbooks, Robert begins to attend some entrepreneurial training sessions. He begins to read success books. He takes time out of his schedule to learn new skill—things like selling, and how to work with other people. All of these things take Robert out of his comfort zone, but it fills his quiver with new arrows. These arrows help him hit his target and change his life.

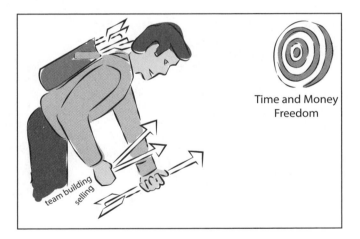

Time and Money Freedom

Folks, it is time for you to become aware that almost all of modern culture is focusing on the arrows, and not the targets. Sure, go ahead and build up a skill set and put those arrows in your quiver. Do the things you like doing and get better at them. But, don't go running around with a bunch of arrows, go out and look for great targets. Once you find the target that is truly worthy of your life endeavor, fill your quiver with the right kinds of arrows.

MISTAKE

4

Doing The Things You Hate Doing First, Instead Of Paying Someone Else To Do Them

Let's keep this one short and sweet, because I hate writing about it. (Just kidding.) We are going to keep it short because this is a very easy mistake to make, and a very easy mistake to stop.

I hate to cut the grass. I just hate it. When we lived in Las Vegas, our community took care of cutting the grass. But, when my wife and I moved to Orlando, we bought a house without a community lawn care service.

"Are you going to buy a lawn mower?" Jeanne asked me. My reply was typical. I couldn't just say a simple, "No" because I am an author, who is always looking for a great thing to write about later. I said, "No, if I buy a lawn mower, I will have to use it someday, and I hate cutting grass. You see, if I cut the grass, it will take me five hours: one hour to actually cut it and four hours to complain about it."

I went on to explain, "If I pay someone else to cut it, I really don't care how long it takes for that person to do it."

Of course, by that time, Jeanne had walked away and was doing something else, muttering to herself saying something like, "Why can't he just give me a simple *no* instead of going on and on…" (I couldn't hear the rest.)

Hire Hal to Do The Things You Hate to Do

What was my solution to the grass-cutting problem in Orlando? I hired a man named Hal to cut the grass. Hal had a big truck and trailer. He had a guy to help him. Hal would show up every week, year-round. (Hey, this was Orlando. Grass really grows fast in Orlando.) Hal was always cheerful when cutting my grass. Why wouldn't he be? Hal LIKED cutting grass. And do you know why he liked cutting grass? He liked it because I PAID him to cut it. He was working for himself. He didn't have a boss looking over his shoulder.

Hal would periodically *upsell* me on something, like a yearly clean up, or fertilizer or something. It always made the yard look better. It made ME look better!

What Was Hal Selling Me?

I wasn't paying Hal to cut the grass. I was paying him to cut the grass so that I could write books. Did I mention before that I HATE cutting grass and that it would take me five hours (one hour cutting/four hours complaining)? In those five hours, how much money could I make writing books? I can tell you this, it was a LOT more than it cost me to hire Hal.

What was Hal selling me? He sold me the opportunity to write enough books to keep Jeanne home from work for 19 years when our kids were growing up. He sold me the time to pay for a car, with cash. He sold me the time to help put my kids through school. He sold me the time so that I could go on vacation and not worry about my yard. He sold me… well, you get the picture.

Why Do You Hate Doing The Things You Hate Doing?

Why do I hate cutting the grass? Who knows? I guess because it is boring, and because it always needs cutting again. Why do you hate doing the things that you hate doing? Maybe you find them boring, or maybe because you never seem to have time to do them, or maybe because it takes you away from something you really LIKE to do.

Everyone has a reason for hating to do something. And, the reason really doesn't matter. The fact is, if you hate doing something, you are never going to be really good at doing it. If you are never really good at doing it, you are going to hate it. It is a vicious circle.

So Why Do Time Managers Say Things Like, "Do The Things You Hate Doing First?"

Time management experts are always telling you to do the things you hate doing first, and then do the things you like doing. It seems really stupid to me. If you hate doing something, why do it? If it really bothers you, how much is it costing you in monetary and emotional strain to do it?

When should you do the things you hate doing? How about *NEVER*, does *NEVER* work for you? It works for me—and so does Hal. (Well, Hal is long gone. We live on an island community now, and we have a different Hal. But the "new Hal" still works for me. And I still hate cutting grass, although I have not cut grass in over forty years.)

What If the Thing You Hate Doing is Your JOB?

For some people, the thing they hate doing the most is their job. They just absolutely hate it. This is a terrible situation. It makes me sad every time I hear about it. I just can't imagine getting up each morning and trudging off to work, only to hate every minute of it, all day long. I just can't imagine how that person comes home from work, exhausted and angry, and then tries to have a home life. It makes me very, very sad to think about it.

So, What Does That Person Do?

I already told you that I don't like it when time management experts say things like, "Do the things you hate doing first, and then do the thing you like doing last." And I also really hate it when so-called experts say things like, "If you hate your job (or some other thing you hate to do) then you have to start finding things that make that job bearable. Maybe it is thinking about what you are going to do with the money, or how special it makes you feel that only you can do something so difficult, or…" Forgive me, but I just HATE IT when people talk like that. But, we hear it all the time.

Folks, if you hate something, change it! Don't try to make it work out somehow. Don't put a brave face on it. Change it.

It might take you YEARS to change it. You might have to do some really tough things in order to change it, but you MUST do those tough things.

Life is just too short, and too precious to waste doing things you hate doing. If you hate doing your job, take advantage of all the other income-producing opportunities that are around today. There is absolutely no excuse for sticking with something that you hate. You will never be good at it, and it will make you sad all the time. And then, I will hear about it, and it will make me sad as well.

Start Over – On The Side

If you hate your job, start making money on the side. You will be amazed at how much better this will make you feel. Why do people hate their jobs? Well, in many cases it is because they feel trapped. They wouldn't mind their jobs so much if they were not so dependent on that job. They would find it a lot easier to work for a crazy boss if they could just *laugh* about it and not have to take it so seriously. (Take it from me. I know what I am talking about! I have a really nice boss now, but in the past, I had some real crazies. If I wasn't making a lot of money on the side, it would have been very unpleasant to think that my boss had control over me. Instead, I was able to just laugh it off, because I had a separate source of income.)

Here is something I know for a fact: crazy bosses love it when they know you have no choice! If you hate your job, make sure your job is not controlling your life. Change. Grow.

Start thinking about the things you hate doing, and start doing something about it. You don't like walking the dog? Pay someone else to do it. You don't like doing the wash, or cleaning the house? Pay someone else to do it.

It is all a matter of changing yourself. You need to become aware that the mistake of doing the things you hate doing is YOUR mistake. You don't have to do them at all. Just hire Hal.

MISTAKE

5

Trying To Fill A Leaky Barrel, Instead of Building Tall, Solid Staves

I really love talking about this mistake, because the graphics are so great! I am about to show you a really amazing concept—one that is absolutely critical to your success. And, I am going to give you a few concepts to think about. But, and this is really great news, I am also going to show you a picture that explains the whole concept in a split-second of realization. In fact, I think you are going to get a B.G.O. from this mistake.

What Is a B.G.O.?

The B.G.O. is a *blinding glimpse of the obvious*. I clearly remember the day I heard this expression. I was doing a workshop for a small hotel chain. They had all their top executives there. I showed them the picture that I am about to share with you, and the owner of the hotel chain said, "I just had a B.G.O." In other words, what I was saying became so obvious to the attendees—just because it was accompanied by a simple drawing that no one could dispute.

So, are you ready for your B.G.O.?

Okay, here it is. Take a look at this picture, and think about this: A barrel can only hold water up to the level of the lowest stave. Therefore, if you have a "success barrel," and one of your important elements is not as tall as the others, you can never attain a high level of success.

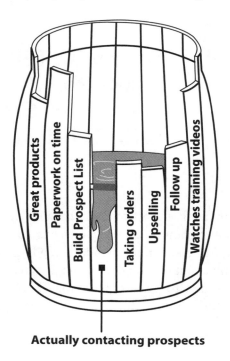

Actually contacting prospects

No B.G.O. Yet?

What's that? You have not yet had your B.G.O.? Okay, no problem. Let's talk about it and see how you feel in a few pages. I am about to give you some really valuable information that will help you "get this" concept. You will be amazed at how simple it is, and how you can use this barrel example to give people a B.G.O. in all kinds of settings and endeavors.

But First, My Personal B.G.O. Story

A few years ago, I was on the Board of Directors for our church. The board members were asked to help "grow our church." We hired a consultant, and he shared some fabulous observations about mistakes that many churches make. As it turns out, those same observations apply to "growing" almost any kind of organization, business, or person. In fact, in the years since learning about this process, I have used it to grow my personal business.

First, However, Let's Learn About Barrels

To understand the power of what that church consultant told us, you need to first understand how to construct a barrel. Barrels are made up of vertical pieces of wood called "staves." You place the staves side-by-side, and use barrel hoops to hold them in place. When the barrel is strong and secure, you can fill it up with water (or whatever else you want to put in there).

Take a look at that picture of the barrel again. It shows a barrel that has various sizes of staves. Some staves are taller than others. But, it really doesn't matter how tall the tallest staves are. What really matters is how short the shortest stave is, because the barrel can *only be filled with water up to the level of the shortest stave!* Are you beginning to see something useful here?

When I first saw this demonstration at our church, the consultant asked us to name some of the most important things about our church. We came up with things like: strong faith, great leaders, warm and friendly community, children's programs, etc. The consultant asked us if we excelled in each of these areas. We, of course, recognized that we did not. At that point, he did something very impressive. He asked us to assign a name to each of our staves in the barrel. We named one stave "children's programs," and another one, "warm and friendly community," etc. In other words, each of the staves was named for something that we felt was important to foster church growth.

Now, I am not going to spend time here going over which staves we felt were shorter, and which ones were stronger. But, as he pointed out, "Water could only rise to the level of the lowest stave." In other words, if we had a weakness, it made it impossible for us to fill up the barrel!

How Does This Apply to You and Your Mistakes?

You can probably see where this is going, can't you? We can use the barrel analogy for our personal success-building, wealth-generating, relationship-making journey, can't we? We need to decide which factors are the most important aspects of our lives (the ones that will most likely help us achieve success) and then we must make sure that EACH ONE OF THEM IS AS TALL AS THE BEST OF THEM in order to fill up our barrels with water (wealth/success/love/etc.).

How Is This Different, and What Is The Mistake People Are Making?

Too many people simply ignore their weaknesses, and concentrate on their strengths. This is okay if your weaknesses are minor, and do not contribute much to your goals and dreams. For example, if one of your weaknesses is, "not a good cook" well... you may be going hungry at times, but it probably doesn't matter much to your wealth-building success. (Of course, if you are a restaurant owner, this could be a VERY bad weakness.)

However, what if one of your weaknesses is, "relationships with business partners"? Well, that one, ladies and gentlemen, could be a real problem!

Does this happen in real life? Are there people out there who are not good with some things so they concentrate on the things they like and feel good about? Of course there are!

Let me give you two examples that I hear all the time.

1. "I don't like to ask people for their business, so I concentrate on other things, like writing great reports. I get all my paperwork in on time, every time." This person is going to have a barrel that has a very high "paperwork done on time" stave, but a very low "closes sales and creates income" stave. When this person tries to fill their barrel up, it will only rise to the level of the top of the weakest stave. They aren't going to do very well, are they?

2. Now, what about the person who is not good at analytical tasks like calculating profit margins? Have you ever heard someone like that say something like the following? "I am not good with numbers, so I concentrate on my people skills." Again, this person is going to have a problem. They are going to have a low stave, and whatever they are trying to fill the barrel with is going to run out over the top of that stave and be lost.

Does This Mean That You Have to Be Perfect At Everything?

Right now, I know at least some of my readers are saying, "Well, I might as well give up. I am not great at everything I need to do in order to be successful. I might as well give up right now and save myself the trouble." Are you saying that or thinking it right now? If so, then stop worrying. Let me explain something that is GREAT news for people who think like that.

- Don't use the "I am not perfect" excuse. You don't have to be perfect at everything.

- Remember, the barrel can only be filled up to the lowest stave, right? But, unless you are absolutely terrible, no, make that *excruciatingly* horrible at something, you can at least fill up the barrel to the height of the lowest stave, right? This means that you might not be able to achieve absolutely flawless success, but you can at least achieve some success. Don't use the barrel example as an excuse to quit. Use it as an incentive later when you realize that you have gone as far as you can go without changing.

- You can change and grow. As you embark on your success journey (in whatever endeavor), you can always get started and build your success without much change or growth. In fact (and this is important) you often don't know what your weaknesses are until you get started! I mean, after all, if you are doing something brand new, something out of your comfort zone, how can you possibly know what you need to work on for success?

- However, as you begin to grow your success, start thinking about the things that are keeping your barrel from filling to the top. Instead of ignoring these things, (as many people make the mistake of doing) you can make a decision to grow and change yourself. This is a remarkable time in your personal success journey.

- In the end, you need to be the "whole package" in order to succeed fully. But in the beginning, you just have to get started! You will figure it out as you go along.

Let's Look At That Mistake Again

Almost everyone I ever worked with, and almost every student I ever taught, told me that they were not good at certain things. It was amazing. They were *always* saying it. And they never caught on to the idea that they would have to *change* some of those things in order to be successful in life.

We all need to learn what things are important in the success-building, barrel-filling process, and then become accomplished at each of them. There is, unfortunately, no way around it. You need to be the whole person, not a part of the whole person.

A Few F.A.Q. for the Barrel Concept:

1. Why can't I just ignore my weaknesses if I have some remarkable strengths?

   Well, just take a look at that barrel. Did you miss the B.G.O.? It doesn't matter how strong your strengths are when you are trying to accomplish something really BIG. You can only fill that barrel to the height of the lowest stave.

2. "I was always told that I just had to do my best. Isn't that good enough?"

Well, no. If it were good enough, you would already have what you want out of life. (Another B.G.O.)

3. Why can't I just find a team member who is good at the things that I am not good at, and build a barrel with him/her?

   Would you be anxious to be on a team with someone who has a leaky barrel? And, what if that team member decides to grow and change? Aren't they going to get tired of carrying your water?

4. How do I know what I need to have in order to build my barrel?

   Just look at what successful people are doing, and build the same barrel!

5. This sounds really difficult. Are there ANY shortcuts to building a tall, success-generating barrel?

   Absolutely. There are two of them:

   1. Join a *system* and just do what they suggest. When you buy into a system, you are getting a series of tall, strong, success-holding staves. All you need to do is to be smart enough to put some hoops around them and start filling!

   2. Simply *duplicate* the successful people in your system. That's all you need to do. Do exactly what they are doing.

MISTAKE

6

Listening To Poor Teachers Instead Of Learning From Rich Buyers

Okay, this is going to be very controversial, but if you take the time to read this chapter, and let the message sink in, it will be a real game changer for you. Some of you, however, are going to think that I am "talking trash" about a whole group of well-meaning, dedicated people. Indeed, somebody is sure to tell the people that I work with that I am saying bad things about teachers. You see, I am a college professor, and this is going to sound like I am being disrespectful towards the very institutions I serve.

But, if you do find yourself getting angry at what I am about to tell you in this chapter, please read "Seeing with your eyes instead of seeing with your brain." (Mistake #9) In that chapter, I talk about using your brain to *translate* the input your eyes and ears get. So, in this chapter, I want you to put that advice to work. I want you to carefully read what I am about to lay out for you, and before you *react*, look for the truth in what I am telling you.

I Am Not Disrespecting Teachers and Professors

I am going to say some tough things in this chapter. They are tough because they are true. I am going to show you how our educational system is teaching each and every one of us to fail. You see, in order to pass all your courses and subjects, you have to give your teachers and professors the right answer. You know how it works, right? You take tests, or write papers, or do projects. Your teachers always, always *grade* those assignments. Have you ever turned in an assignment or taken a test and NOT received a grade for it? In fact, if you did all the work to get a good grade, and you do not receive any grade, aren't you angry? What about if you do a lot of hard work to master a subject, and someone else does almost nothing? Yet, both of you receive the same grade. How does that make you feel?

You see, the system of assigning grades sets us up for a lifetime of worrying about what other people will think of our work and effort. It puts us in the perpetual position of being judged for everything we do. And, that feeling of being judged carries over into our money-making efforts. It carries over into our relationships. It is a huge weight that is tied around our necks and keeps us from becoming free. And those weights are put there by our relationships with our teachers.

I First Started To Notice This When...

Let me tell you about the other authors I help, because that is when I really began to notice this particular problem. Folks, after writing over twenty books, many of them international best-sellers, and being named to both the *Independent Book Publishers Hall of Fame* and the *Self-Published Authors Hall of Fame*, I had a lot of would-be authors who were asking me for help. I would get phone calls and emails, asking me for advice, or to review their manuscripts. For a while, I did my best to answer all the questions. However, as the demands grew, I started charging people for my time with them. This had one immediate effect: the number of people who wanted my help suddenly dropped off substantially! (Okay, I learned a great lesson there. If you want to make money from your expertise, charge for it. It "weeds out" the people who are not serious!)

However, even the serious authors I was working with (for excellent money!) seemed to suffer from the effects of our education system. I had really interesting, highly accomplished and successful people who were afraid to put their books into print. Why? Because they wanted to do, "Just one more edit."

In other words, these people would put all their time into writing a book, and then not publish it because they were afraid of the "grade" they would get—not for the content of the book, but for the way it was written. It actually paralyzed them. They just couldn't let that book out.

There was another important, I-need-to-get-approval-first impact on the success of these writers. I was a self-published author. All of my successful books came right out of my mind, and into the hands of the readers who wanted them (and needed them.) But, the authors I was working with all wanted to "get a real publisher." They were appalled whenever I told them to just go ahead and publish it themselves. You see, they couldn't get past that approval stage. They wanted someone (like an expert or a teacher) to *tell them that their book was good*; instead of putting it out there and letting the *buyers* tell them that the book was exactly what they needed. It would drive me crazy.

I had one woman who said to me, "My dream is to see my book in the bookstores." I had two pieces of advice for her:

1. If you want to see your book in a bookstore, you had better hurry! Bookstores are going out of business!

2. Why is your dream to see your book in the bookstores? Perhaps your dream should be to see your book in the hands of *buyers* and then to see their money in your bank account!

There Is A Difference Between Subjects And Success

Folks, teachers are subject experts. (This is especially true for professors.) They know a certain subject, and they are great at teaching it to you. Math teachers and professors know how to teach you to add, subtract, multiply and divide—for everything except MONEY. English teachers and professors are experts at teaching you how to speak correctly, and to communicate with perfect diction—except they forget to tell you that angry people don't listen to you no matter what you say or how you say it! Science teachers and professors are excellent at teaching you the rules of chemistry, but do nothing to tell you how to create real chemistry between you and people who want what you have.

But, We Need To Know These Things

I am not saying you don't need to know these things. I am just saying that you have to turn off that teacher's voice inside of you that says things have to be done a certain way. Yes, if you are an engineer or an architect, we want you to remember what the professor said about building a strong bridge over that deep gorge, but for goodness sake, stop hearing those "teacher voices" in your head when it comes to your personal success! Your personal success is based on your ability to attract other people to you, to discover what they need and want, and then to give it to them! And then to give it to them again and again!

And, if you *really* want to be successful, you need to set up systems that will allow you to stop working so hard. You need systems that will *keep* those buyers coming back again and again—without you having to do the same job again and again.

It Might Be A Matter Of Philosophy

One of my relatives is a very successful businessman. He is also on the Advisory Board for the Business School at a prestigious university. He told me that many companies are now looking to hire *Philosophy* majors for their business units, instead of MBA graduates. Why? It turns out that the Philosophy Majors have been trained to *solve problems creatively* and the MBA students are trained to *solve problems by applying theory*. Can you believe it? Imagine that! It turns out that being able to *think outside the box* is often more successful than knowing exactly where the box is and what's inside it! You see, the Philosophy Majors received some basic training, and then they were turned loose to observe, build relationships between people and producers, and then to solve problems with new, creative ideas. It turns out that no one had told them *what the solution should be*, so the philosophers were free to come up with new solutions—without the limits imposed by being married to a theory.

Now I should tell you, I am not a Philosophy professor. In fact, I teach business courses. So I am free to say the things I am saying, because I can never be accused of selling Philosophy as a major.

It Turns Out That It Isn't The Teacher...

It's the student that matters. Don't be trapped by what you learned in school. Be freed by it. Be free to stand on the platform of knowledge that you received, and then freely apply it to solve your problems, and the problems of others. Forget your teachers. They had their purpose in your life. Now it is time to look ahead, and to do the things you need to do. Forget the "rules" for the things you learned (unless you are building a bridge or an airplane!) and start using the *process* of learning to build something meaningful in your life, without worrying about what your teachers would say.

Do You Really Want What Teachers Have?

Look, here is something to think about. Almost all teachers are poor. That's right – poor. Did you ever hear someone say, "I can't wait to grow up and be a teacher so I can drive a really nice car, and build a beautiful home"? I don't think I ever heard of that, and I am a teacher!

When I first became a professor, it wasn't for the money. It was for the *time*. I was in the restaurant business, and it was a lot of work day after day, weekends, nights, etc. But, when I went back to school and got my Master's Degree, and then my Doctoral Degree, I discovered just how much easier it was to be a professor than a chef. I loved the extra time I had, and I loved not having a bunch of hungry and thirsty customers who wanted to eat and drink at exactly the same hours I didn't want to work. Even more than that, when I became a professor, I suddenly didn't have all those crazy employees working for me, depending on me for their income. But, I also didn't have much money! And that bothered me, because I still wanted the same things out of my work income: a nice car, vacations, a good home, etc.

It was ironic. There I was, teaching students how to make money (remember, I am in a school of business) and I didn't have any. The people around me didn't have any. Yet, there we were, giving our students assignments and giving them grades for the work they did. If they listened to us exactly, and gave us the "right answers" then they got a good grade. If they didn't, they got a bad grade.

And what was going through my mind all that time? It was the voice of the teachers and professors I had. They were looking over my shoulder, grading me. I was passing on the same lessons to my students that my teachers had passed on to me a generation earlier.

What Changed?

Simple, I wanted money—a LOT more money. And, I realized that to get that money, I had to stop listening to those teachers who were looking over my shoulder from the past. I had to disregard all the useless rules and theories that had built up in me. Instead, I had to figure out where the money was, and then go get it. And, I wanted to do that without giving up my time. After all, I LOVED all the time I had as a professor. I just didn't like the money!

How Did I Change?

Okay, get ready for perhaps the biggest lesson in this entire book. Are you ready? Here it is:

1. I wanted to have more money.

2. I figured out who had my money—other people.

3. I discovered the secret to getting other people to give me *their* money so that it would become *my* money.

4. The secret is this: Those people didn't care if I wrote, did math, or even THOUGHT like my teachers did.

5. All those people cared about is that I could solve their problems. They didn't care HOW I solved those problems – they just wanted them solved.

And, when I stopped thinking about what poor people had taught me, and started concentrating on what rich people were teaching me, everything worked out. I soon started making more money—a LOT more money.

I Still Had Teachers – But They Were RICH Teachers

Folks, I started listening to two groups of people: rich, successful business people, and rich successful buyers. It turns out that both groups had problems I could solve. And, both groups would give me money if I could solve their problems.

What Problems Did They Have, and Why Would They Teach Me?

I'm telling you, get ready to learn something really valuable here. This is BIG, BIG, BIG!

1. Rich, Successful Business People

    a. Their problem – they wanted to be even more successful, and they didn't want to work more hours to be more rich and successful

    b. Why they would teach me – they wanted me to learn to make money so they would make even more money. Therefore, they were willing to teach me how to do it.

2. Rich Buyers

    a. Their problem – they had money (from working hard) and they had problems. They were willing to give me money if I could solve their problems.

    b. Why they would teach me – If they thought I was really interested in their problems, they were willing to spend some time teaching me about their problem, so that I could solve it for them in the best way possible. And, they were willing to pay me while they were teaching me.

Did ANY Teacher Ever Teach You This?

Of course they did not. The schools and universities where they work are just not set up to do this. That's okay, they do teach you a lot of good stuff. But, like I said before, you simply have to stop worrying about what those poor teachers taught you—immediately after graduating. You need to start thinking about what rich people can teach you. And believe me, rich people can teach you a lot.

But what is even more important is that you realize that rich people are excited about teaching you things, because they get more out of it than any regular teacher you ever had. If you start learning from rich business people, they will make more money when you learn to make more money. If you start learning from rich buyers, they will get what they want, while you get what YOU want.

Isn't that better than getting an "A" in a paper? Isn't that better than getting a gold star on your test?

You bet it is!

MISTAKE

7

Looking For The Corners Of The Puzzle, Instead Of Looking At The Picture On The Box

Let's Kick This One Off With a Story

A woman is out shopping when her husband calls her on her cell phone. "I need some help," said the husband. "I just found this jigsaw puzzle in the cabinet, and I am having the worst time trying to put it together."

"What seems to be the problem?" asks the wife.

"I dumped out all the pieces, and they all look exactly the same. This thing is impossible."

"Did you try looking at the picture on the box?" she asks.

"Yes," came the reply. "It is a picture of a tiger. He is wearing a bandanna around his neck."

"I know what the problem is," says the exasperated woman. "You found a box of Frosted Flakes."

Okay, so this is a little on the *corny* side, but let's face it, many of us miss the obvious when we are trying to solve a puzzle. And, the puzzle doesn't have to be a commercially produced box of cardboard shapes. We try to solve all kinds of puzzles in our lives. Every day, we are presented with opportunities and options, problems, and challenges.

Each of them has many pieces to it. It is up to us how we want to put it all together.

Here is the Problem

For most of us, there are a lot of messy situations in life. It doesn't matter if it is a challenge or an opportunity, the number of jumbled pieces can sometimes be overwhelming. Forget about the Frosted Flakes example above, and think of your challenges and opportunities as a jigsaw puzzle. Imagine someone dumping it out on your desk, with no picture. You look at the jumbled pile of pieces, all different shapes and sizes, and think, "I don't even know where to start!"

- Some people just stop right there. They give up. It is such a mess that they don't even know how to choose the first piece.

- Other people look for the "corner pieces." It is often easier to identify these pieces, because they have a distinctive shape. They stand out from the rest of the pieces.

- Other people look for all the pieces that have a straight edge on them. They assume that these are the "border pieces." They think, "Okay, if I can just get the outline done, maybe it will be possible to fill in the middle."

But, even if you have a strategy, looking for the corner pieces for example, it is still almost impossible to put together a complicated puzzle, with HUNDREDS of pieces, if you do not have a picture to go by. If there were no picture, how would you possibly know how to begin, let alone finish?

Okay, Enough of the Metaphors, Please Solve This Puzzle

At this point, I might say to you, "Okay, you get the picture…" But maybe you don't. After all, there is no picture yet, right?

Folks, let me fit the pieces together for you about this mistake. We have already established that your life is full of puzzles. We also established that there are *some* strategies you can use to put the puzzle together without a picture to guide you, but it is still very difficult. In fact, many, many people will spend quite a bit of time trying to piece it together without a picture, only to give it up.

And, we all know that it is MUCH easier to solve a puzzle if you have a picture to go by, right? So, what am I saying? I am saying to put your life's goals into a clear, easy-to-understand picture, and THEN try to solve the problems and puzzles.

What Is The Picture?

Your picture is your dream. Your picture is what you want your life to be. When it gets messy, when someone dumps a big pile of confusing pieces in front of you, you will always have your dream picture to guide you on how to put it all together.

Let's look at two examples. One is a challenge, and the other is an opportunity.

The Challenge – A co-worker is spreading gossip about someone else in the office. The gossip may, or may not be true, but it is going to hurt the reputation of that other person. You look at your desk, and there is a big pile of pieces there. You want to learn if the gossip is true. You would love to run and tell someone else about it. You really don't care for the person everyone is gossiping about. In fact, that person was just spreading some lies about another person in the office, and it might be fun to see them get "what's coming to them."

The Picture – One of your goals in life is to be fair and respectful of others. You want to be seen as that kind of person. It is important to you. It is part of your brand. You want others to respect you for your fairness and kindness. It is a picture in your mind.

Solving the Puzzle – With this picture firmly in mind, is there any way that you will put up with gossip? If you *spread* gossip, it will not fit into your picture, right? For that matter, even *listening* to gossip is not going to be a piece of that picture.

Problem Solved – Build your picture piece by piece. *Each and every piece of your puzzle* is important. Walk away from the gossiper, and make it clear that you do not want to be part of it, ever.

Now, Let's Look At An Opportunity Puzzle

The Opportunity – A young couple is approached by some friends. "We have something we would like to share with you," say the friends. "It is a business opportunity, and it would be great to get your opinion on it. Would you be willing to watch a ten-minute video? We will call you afterwards to answer any questions you have." The young couple is intrigued, but cautious. They are both very busy at work, and they want to start a family, so they are very concerned about getting into anything new at this point. But, they trust their friends, and they know that they would only have approached them if they thought it was a good thing. They watch the video, and they get excited. Later, on the phone, they ask questions, and their friends introduce them to a successful person from the business. But, even after asking questions, the young couple is still not exactly sure if this is going to be the right thing for them.

The Picture – The young couple are real planners. They *know* that they want more out of life than what the average people are getting. For example, the young woman wants to spend time at home with her children when they come along. Right now, they need both incomes to make ends meet. They have a firm picture in their minds about what they want to do in life, and how they want to spend their time and talents.

Solving the Puzzle – It doesn't take long for this couple to realize that the business opportunity they are looking at contains the "missing pieces" of the puzzle of their lives! If the woman is to stay home with the children, it means they need to replace an income – and do it in a way that still gives them "time freedom." These missing pieces complete the puzzle.

Problem Solved – In the example of the "Challenge Puzzle," we stated, "each piece of the puzzle is critical." When you are solving a puzzle by looking at the picture, the center pieces are just as important as the corner pieces. And, in the case of the "opportunity puzzle," all the pieces are important as well—especially the "missing pieces" that can prevent you from solving the puzzle. This couple had a picture of how they wanted to live. That picture showed the woman staying at home with the young children. Without the new business opportunity, their puzzle was missing some pieces. With the opportunity, they could complete the picture of their puzzle.

Without a solid picture to go by, you have to rely on second-rate strategies for solving all the puzzles in your life. As you become aware of this mistake, you will slowly *get the picture*!

You know you are going to have puzzles in life. Everyone gets them. So, create your dream picture now, and you will always have a head start on putting all the pieces into place. More importantly, you will know if any of the pieces are missing.

MISTAKE

8

Renting To Own Instead Of Owning To Rent

Most people spend their entire lives renting. Oh, they may think that they own things like their cars or their homes, but how many people have paid cash for those things, or have paid off the loans that they use to buy them? And, if they do pay them off, what do they do? They buy a new car, or a new home, and start the renting all over again.

Renting to own is not only a mistake – it is a dangerous mistake. What makes it so dangerous? It is so dangerous because most people are never aware of the consequences of renting to own. They think to themselves *everyone else is doing this,* and so it must be the thing to do.

A Bad Rental Story

Here is a great story from my audio book, "Do You Own Your Own Life Or Are You Just Renting?" A very successful and wealthy businessman had an uncle that he just loved. This man would do anything for his uncle. But, the man was so often away on business trips that he very rarely got to see his favorite relative. When his uncle finally died, the man wanted to make sure that he gave his uncle a fantastic send-off. He called the funeral director and said, " I don't care how much it costs. I want you to give my Uncle Bob a great funeral – one that everyone will remember."

Of course, just before the funeral, the wealthy businessman got called out of town on yet another business trip. He was reluctant to go, but he had the solace of knowing that he had spent a lot of money on his uncle's funeral, and everyone was going to admire it. While on the trip, he got a report from other relatives that the funeral was indeed fantastic. Everyone kept saying, "Your Uncle Bob would have loved this. What a great tribute to him."

Thirty days after the funeral, the businessman got the bill from the funeral director. It was for $30,182.50. His first thought was, "That sure is a lot of money, but I did tell him to spend whatever it takes. And, everyone is saying that Uncle Bob would've loved it. I guess it was worth it." He paid the bill.

Another thirty days later, and he got a surprise in the mail. The funeral director had sent him another bill for $182.50. The man was perplexed, but he was so busy that he just decided to pay it and not worry about it. One month later, the same thing happened, and he paid it again.

This went on for about six months, and the businessman was getting very angry. Finally, he had a few minutes of spare time and he called the funeral director. "Why do I keep getting this bill for $182.50 every month?" he asked. The funeral director had an immediate answer. "You said you wanted him to have a first-class funeral, right?"

"Yes," said the businessman. "But what does that have to do with this bill that keeps coming in every month for $182.50?"

"Well," said the funeral director. "We knew it would be important for your uncle to look good at his funeral. Everyone would be staring at him. So, we rented him a tuxedo."

What's Your Bad Rental Story?

Okay, so maybe you haven't rented a tuxedo for your dead uncle, but I can guarantee you that you are probably living in "Full Rental Mode." Let's prove it to you. Look at your checking account. How many checks do you write each month for recurring bills? Your home and your car payments are the first obvious things you will spot. But, there are more. You pay insurance? Do you have loans for your education or your kids' education? All these things add up, and they put you in debt, which is just a form of rent.

But wait, it gets worse. What about your credit cards? Do you pay them off every month? Do you carry a balance? Did you know that the average family in the United States has a credit card debt balance of over $8,000? Isn't that insane? And that's just for the *average*! As one of my clients once told me after hearing about the average credit card debt, "Well, at least I'm above average in something!"

But it gets even more awful. The vast majority of people are involved in a form of "rent to own" with their jobs. That's right. You are going into debt with your job: time debt. Here's how it works. You get a job, and your boss pays you money each week. In order to get that money, you have to give up your time. Every day, five days a week, 50 weeks a year, you are at that office, or behind the counter, or on the road.

You have no equity on your job. You don't own a single thing about it. In effect, you are renting space at work, and they pay you a lot less money than your time is worth—simply because they are the ones who own everything. You are renting your right to work.

If you get a $5,000 a year raise, what do you do? Do you use that money to pay down your debt? Do you use that money to buy yourself out of debt and into freedom? No, most people take on more debt when they get a raise. They say, "Well, I will have this money coming in every week now. Now, I can afford to buy more things on credit." They get another car, or renovate their home, or refinance it, or even buy a new house. Every time they make a little more money, they enter into more debt. In other words, they rent even more things, more expensive things, which keeps them in time debt and renting space at their job.

Why Do So Many People Do This?

They do it *because that is what we do*. It is what we're taught to do. Enough said on that score.

Why Aren't You Aware Of This?

You aren't aware of this because everyone is telling you how much sense it makes. Everyone around you is doing it. You are taught how to do this in school. Your parents pass it on to you. You teach your kids to do this. You are building a life of debt and rent instead of a life of equity.

But, if you really want to become aware of it, all you have to do is start looking at your spending habits. Go ahead. Take out that checkbook. Start to track things on the computer. Use your mobile phone apps to track your spending.

How long have you financed your car? Is it for 60 months? Maybe you don't even own your car. Maybe you lease your car. Either way, it is renting.

How long is the term of your mortgage on your house? Is it for 30 years? How old are you now? Do you really think that you're going to pay off your home, and then live there happily ever after? Most people don't. Most people end up selling their homes and buying a new one, well before their mortgages are paid. Many people refinance their homes to take out the equity and then spend that equity as down payments for more debt!

But, because that's what everyone is doing, it looks like it is the right thing to do. People tell themselves, "Well, I am building equity."

Decision – Build Equity And Then Rent It To Others!

I have some great news. It is not difficult to overcome the "rent to own" cycle. All you need to do is to build equity, and then use that equity to make money. Then you "own to rent."

Would you like a couple of examples of how to build equity and then use it as "own to rent" money-making machine? Here are just a couple of examples:

1. Set money aside, and invest in the stock market. Stocks are equity. You own a piece of a company. Everyone knows this,

but most people never put money aside for a retirement fund. However, it is one of the easiest ways to build equity. You see, when you own a company's stock, you are renting your money to them. This is what I mean when I say, "Own to rent."

2. Buy some investment properties and rent them to tenants. How can you afford a rental property? All you need to do is to save up the down payment, and then take a mortgage. Do your math. Make sure that the amount of rent you get will pay off the mortgage. Can you see how this is owning to rent? You have two kinds of ownership equity here. First, you have equity in the house. Second, you have an asset that other people pay you for. At the end of 30 years, you own the house—and all the equity in it. This is true owning to rent entrepreneurship.

3. Build a distribution channel for a company that wants to move its products. Hundreds of thousands of companies are looking for customers. Did you realize that you can "own to rent" a fabulous, money-generating distribution channel? This is one of the least expensive, most hassle-free ways to build equity. This is "owning to rent" on steroids!

Just Get Started

Owning to rent isn't difficult. But first, come to grips with the fact that most of your life has been spent renting to own. Once you build this awareness, start taking immediate steps to build equity. Use that equity to generate income. Once you let your money work for you, you will stop working for money. You will begin to own things—really own them. Don't get trapped in the "give me a raise and I will buy something more" merry-go-round. Let someone else pay the rent!

MISTAKE

9

Seeing With Your Eyes (Or Your Ears) Instead Of With Your Brain

Who is your favorite rapper and hip-hop star? Mine is Kris Parker, otherwise known as "KRS-One." Actually, I had never heard of KRS-One until I decided to write about the mistake "Seeing with your eyes…" It seems that the rapper used similar lyrics on his album's top song. The lyrics came up when I did a Google search to find out who originally said something about "seeing with your eyes…" and, good author that I am, I feel it is only fair to credit the idea to KRS-One. Here are the lyrics that came up on Google:

You know, you don't see with your eyes
You see with your brain
And the more words your brain has
The more things you can see

After reading these lyrics, I thought I better find out something more about Kris Parker before putting the reference into a book that will be viewed by my conservative readers. It turns out that Mr. Parker is an unusual guy. While he originally started out with the typical "gangster rap" of the 1980's, his philosophy changed radically after a close friend and mentor was killed while trying to break up a fight. Now don't get me wrong, I am not going to be an email and text sharing buddy with Parker, in case you're thinking, "What's Quain doing? Has he gone crazy quoting rappers in his books?"

One final note: I found the KRS-One biography in an article from *Rolling Stone* magazine, a publication that once described my best-selling book *Pro-sumer Power* as "The only book I ever wanted to punch in the crotch..." Needless to say, I am not a big fan of Rolling Stone either, but as the man says, "We gotta all get along..." (I actually don't know who said that, but it must have been *the man*. I didn't want to look it up on Google, because I was afraid I would never get this chapter written if I did another search.)

So... Back To Our Mistake!

Look, you don't have to be a rap star to understand what I am saying here. Your eyes (and your ears) are just sensors. Sure, they pick up the images and the sounds, but all they do is transmit those things to your brain. But, here is what you need to know. Everyone *sees and hears* the same things. Images are images and sound is sound. However, it is your BRAIN that processes those inputs into understandable *meaning*. And, everyone interprets the inputs differently, depending on their past experiences, their training and education, and their willingness to put in time and effort into creating understanding.

Wow, That's A Lot To Think About!

You're darn right it is! The trouble is, many people do not take the time to think about it. Instead, they simply look, listen and then respond. If they see something that they don't like, or don't agree with, they dismiss it, or get angry at it. If they hear something, they might ignore it, or forget it. The fact is, we are barraged by so many inputs, all day long, that our brains seem to filter out most of it. It is a protective measure to keep us from overloading; however, it is also a dangerous filter that may keep us from seeing danger or recognizing opportunity.

You Have To Train Your Brain

Words and images are just symbols. You have to *train your brain* to interpret them. It takes time and effort. Look at the words of KRS-One:

"The more words your brain has, the more things you can see."

All I can say to that is "WORD." (You can't see me, but I have my hat turned around backwards, wearing my pants way down on my hips, and holding my fist up to my chest. You should try it.)

Symbols Have Meaning – To You

Try reading this sentence.

Can you read it? I know you can *see* it, but can you understand what it means? It *means* "Buy more of Bill Quain's books." (If you were having trouble it is probably because you forgot to read it from right to left.)

You see (or maybe not), the images are only placeholders for ideas and meaning. It is your brain that does the translating. And, remember this, it isn't just a matter of translating from one language to another, it is a matter of translating *everything that comes into your brain*—into meaningful words for you to see or hear.

You Need Glasses (or hearing aids) For Your *BRAIN*

If your vision starts to get blurry, what do you do? You get glasses. If your hearing starts to diminish, you get hearing aids. Folks, you need to do the same thing for your brain. You need to nourish it and give it tools to make it more clearly understand all the things it has coming into it. How do you do that? You start viewing and listening to positive inputs, and you most **definitely stop letting negative inputs into your brain**. Train your brain by keeping it active. Surround yourself with the good things in life. Be open to new ideas, and when you hear or see them, give them some time. Most importantly, create a huge, vivid dream for yourself and your family, and then *watch and listen* for valuable input that will help you reach your goals.

Reticular Activation :
The Good Stuff Has Been There All Along - You Just Didn't "See" It

In the 1980's (just when KRS-One was turning his negative hip-hop energy into more positive causes) my wife and I bought a Chevy Suburban. What a car! I loved it. But, a funny thing happened when we were driving it home from the dealership. We started seeing Chevy Suburbans *everywhere*. My first thought was, "Wow, did all these people just buy Suburbans?" No, of course they hadn't just bought them. The fact is that these Suburbans were on the road all the time. We just hadn't noticed them. We had seen them with our eyes, but we had not seen them with our brains.

This is called "Reticular Activation."

Folks, when you get a positive, compelling and life-altering dream, you are going to get Reticular Activation at the same time. All of a sudden you are going to start noticing other dreamers, other positive people. You will begin to notice positive books and videos and you will start to let them into your life.

I don't know what the *audio* equivalent of Reticular Activation is, but believe me, when you start allowing positive influences into your brain, positive sounds will start pouring in. Actually, they were pouring in all along, but you just didn't *hear* them, right?

A Great Example

I write positive, dream-building, money-generating, people-building books. So, I train my brain to recognize it when a positive, money-generating, people-growing input comes flooding in. How do you think I got the idea for this chapter? I was sitting around with my "homies" grooving to some very cool rap, when my brother, KRS-One suddenly laid those words on me:

You know, you don't see with your eyes
You see with your brain
And the more words your brain has
The more things you can see

You see, it didn't matter to me where they came from. My brain grabbed on to them and I used them. I hope you can start "seeing and hearing" all the good things around you.

All the good news and positive influence you will ever need is already streaming into your brain. If you are not "seeing nor hearing" them, you are missing one thing—a DREAM. Your dream gives you a reason to stop blocking and start understanding. Your dream will give you Reticular Activation (and whatever the "hearing equivalent" is). You will be amazed when you suddenly realize just how much you have been missing. And you will be amazed at how good it feels to finally *see* your way to your successful future.

Don't rule out great information, just because it is coming from a source that you do not value. More importantly, learn what is valuable, and start watching and listening. Opportunity is there. New ideas are there. Make a decision to find them, recognize them, and use them to make your dream come to life.

"Peace Out"

MISTAKE

10

Solving Quickly Instead Of Stirring Slowly

Okay, it might take you a few minutes to really get this one. You see, most of us are trained to be helpful. It is ingrained in our culture, right? If you see someone who needs your help, aren't you inclined to do something about it, as quickly as you can? What if you see someone in trouble and you just ignore it for a while, hoping it will resolve itself? Would you feel good about that, or bad about that? Most people would definitely feel bad about ignoring someone who is in trouble or pain.

We Are All In The "Helping Business"

Let's take a typical scenario. You are walking down the street, and you see someone who has locked themselves out of their car. They look worried. Maybe they are late for an important appointment. Perhaps they have a sick relative they need to visit. Or maybe, just maybe, it's just some fellow citizen who has a real problem on her hands. What is your natural response? You do what you can to help them, right? You get right in there and do what you can, as quickly as you can.

But what if you are in business? If you see someone with a problem you can solve, what do you do? You jump right in there and solve it. You don't wait. After all, you are in business to make money and here is someone who needs your help. You will solve their problem and this will make them happy, which in turn, will make you happy.

Go to almost any business seminar or workshop and the trainer will say, "To make money, find a need and fill it. You are in the business of solving problems for your customers. If your customer has a problem, solve it right away." Have you heard people say this? I have.

But, I Am Here To Say, "That Is Wrong."

You will not make money-solving problems quickly. You will make money by solving problems s-l-o-w-l-y! The real money is in the slow solution. In a slow solution, you let the people stay in pain longer. This raises the pain to almost unbearable levels. If you try to solve their problem when the pain is small, the amount of money they will give you is small. If you wait, and better yet, if you *stir the pain*, they will give you more money, and it will help them to focus more on your solutions.

I want you to get ready to read some stuff that almost no one is going to tell you. But, believe me, it is where the real money is. It is where true success is.

But First, a Lesson on Focus

When I was a young man, about 17 years old, I was walking on the beach early one morning, in Ocean City, New Jersey. I saw a number of people in the warm water, and decided to take a short swim myself. I was in chest-deep water when I noticed that the undertow was starting to drag me out. It was also dragging out a few of the other people as well, most notably a mother and her teenage daughter.

In those days, we didn't know what a "rip current" was. So, we were not really sure what was happening. Other people were not being towed off shore like we were. It was very strange, but very frightening.

I heard the mother call for help, and I went out to see what I could do. When I got close to them, the mother looked at me with an intense stare, and shoved her daughter into my arms. "Save my daughter," she pleaded. I said, "I have her. She is safe."

What happened next? The mother's face relaxed. She was focused on just one thing: the safety of her daughter. She continued to be pulled out, but that didn't matter so much to her anymore.

Fortunately, I was able to get the daughter out of the rip current and go back to save the mother. Once they were in the shallower water, out of the current, they were fine and I quickly left the beach to go home. That look on her face is still with me today. This woman was focused on one thing. She was committed to her purpose.

This scenario makes the point very well I think. You see, that woman had *pain*. She was *focused*. She was going to stop at nothing to help her daughter because the pain of losing her was so great.

Now, I am not suggesting that you *cause* people pain. What I am saying is this, and it is extremely important if you want to become successful.

"When someone has a problem that you can solve, don't solve the problem immediately. Instead, ask them some questions that will build up the pain. *Stir* that pain with them. Let them get focused on the pain before you try to get them focused on the solution."

Okay, Now You Hate Me

You are probably saying, "Bill, are you nuts? What kind of crazy, sadistic person are you? Are you really telling us that we should make people feel *worse*, instead of making them feel better? Are you really so insensitive?"

Folks, please read this carefully: **I am telling you to make them feel worse FIRST, and then make them feel better.**

An Example

Suppose you are in the vitamin business. You see a co-worker who is feeling tired every afternoon. She is having a hard time staying awake and getting her work done. Your first instinct is to think, "Well, I should tell her about my vitamins. If she takes them, she will be alert and ready to work in the afternoon. This will really help her."

So, you approach her and say, "I have the perfect solution for your problem. Take these vitamins, and you will be wide awake at work, even in the afternoon."

Maybe it will work, and maybe it will not. If it does work, she is going to buy some vitamins. If it doesn't work, it won't matter, because she is going to fall asleep at work anyway, and then get fired, so you won't be looking at her anyway.

(Okay, just kidding about that last part. I am just seeing if you are awake.)

What If You Stirred The Pain?

Okay, let's look at the same situation, but this time, you stir the pain first. Instead of immediately offering a solution, you ask some questions like, "I noticed that you are so tired all the time. That must make it really tough when you go home and your kids need attention. How is that going?"

BANG, you are stirring the pain. You are helping this person to *focus* on the pain—the REAL pain. Sure, she wants to do a better job at work, but what she really wants to focus on is the pain of hurting her family. And, she doesn't want someone to start telling her, "I can solve that." She wants to tell you about how badly she feels about taking quality time away from her family.

Let the pain build. Experience the pain with her. Ask her about how this all makes her feel.

AND THEN share the solution.

Car Salesmen Do It. Politicians Do It.

I am about to show you how YOU have been getting YOUR pain stirred by two groups of individuals: car sales people and politicians. Of course, I realize that this is not what we call an "aspirational" group—meaning that most people don't wake up in the morning and think, "Maybe I will start acting like a car sales person or a politician today. That is something great to *aspire* to." (Nothing against car sales people and politicians, but let's face it, most people aren't crazy about you.)

But think about it. Are you buying cars? Of course. Are you voting for politicians? Of course. Are they stirring your pain – BIG TIME? Here's how:

Car Sales Person – You go to the car dealership to buy a new car. The sales person asks what you want, and then shows you something more expensive. He spends *hours* telling you what a great, dependable car this is. He shows you the *manufacturer's warranty* so that you will feel like you will NEVER have a problem with this car. And then, after selling you the car, he sends you to that back room, "to do the paperwork." What do they do there? They *sell you an extended warranty for that great car that was supposed to be so dependable*! But, first they stir the pain. They say things like, "You just laid out a lot of money for this car. What if the 'such and such' breaks down? Those things cost thousands of dollars, and they aren't covered in the *original*, manufacturer's warranty." MISSION ACCOMPLISHED. PAIN STIRRED. *You pay.*

Politicians – Politicians are MASTERS at stirring pain. After all, you would never vote for them if they didn't stir up the pain. In the United States, we have two political parties, the Republicans and the Democrats. *NOBODY* would vote for a Democrat if they weren't so afraid of the Republicans. *NOBODY* would vote for a Republican if they weren't so afraid that a Democrat would be elected. Who makes you so afraid? The politicians when they stir your pain.

But I Am An Honest Person

Great, but unless you want to leave money on the table, stir the pain. You can be honest and still stir the pain. Stirring the pain is what successful people do, and you know what? The people they come in contact with LOVE them. You see, if you have something that would help me, and I *really* want it, I am so happy that you came along and gave me your understanding. I was in pain, and you were the only one who seemed to understand just how bad the pain was.

Folks, don't be so quick with the solution. Stir the pain.

People don't just want a quick solution. They want to *partner* with people who understand just how bad things are with them. They want to make sure you know just how much pain they are in.

Get to the bottom of the pain. And THEN offer a solution. This works for all kinds of situations—not just in selling people something. Are you in a relationship? Next time, ask about the pain. Don't throw out solutions. Build the relationship by exploring the depths of the suffering. Find out the real problem.

MISTAKE

11

Balancing Risk And Reward – Instead Of Un-Balancing Them!

Risk is what you stand to lose, and reward is what you stand to gain. Now, most people are taught to carefully balance their risks and rewards. In fact, the majority of people spend their whole lives worrying about *losing* something, rather than concentrating on *achieving* something. But, that isn't the big problem and the big mistake I am talking about here.

In life, if you want to be really successful, you want to *un-balance* your risk/reward ratio. In other words, you want to find minimal risks that generate MASSIVE rewards. That is easier than it sounds.

Some Examples

Here is how a typical person invests (gambles) in the stock market. They say things like, "Over time, the stock market has produced an average of 12% return. Therefore, investing in the stock market should make you money over time." (Now, I have heard a lot of estimates of what the stock market SHOULD bring over time. I just used 12% here, because it is a number that I have heard often. It all depends, of course, on which stocks you are investing in, and what time frame we are talking about.)

Let's see what this means. If you invest $1,000, and you receive an average return of 12% per year, you will have $2,000 in 6 years. You will have doubled your money. Most people think that is pretty good, right? And, if you put in another $1,000/year, you will have even more money in 6 years, right?

However, there is a downside. It is quite possible that the 6 years will not have the desired rate of return, right? You could LOSE money over those 6 years, depending on which stocks you pick.

And, that's how most people think about balancing risk and reward. Chances are good that you will not lose all your money. Chances are actually excellent that you will make some money.

But, This is BALANCING Risk and Reward

Your stockbroker is going to ask you a series of questions when you invest. She/he will say things like, "How soon do you need this money?" and "How risky do you want to be with this money?" For example, if you are going to retire in the next ten years, your broker might recommend that you "put your money into something safe." Of course, "something safe" means that your BEST-CASE outcome is going to have low interest with it. You might get a VERY SAFE Government Savings Bond. You will surely not lose any money (unless the Government collapses – highly unlikely) but you will only make about 5% at best.

On the other hand, if you are far from retirement, your broker might say, "Look, you can afford to take on more risk here. You don't need this money for a long time, so why not invest at least some of it in stocks that are riskier, but if they pay off, you will do very well." Have you ever heard of an investment strategy like this? Sure you have. But, what is the meaning of "riskier" and "doing very well?" Here is my understanding of it. If you do poorly in a risky stock investment, you could easily lose it all. If you do well, you could make 20% per year, for a number of years. Again, that seems kind of *balanced*, but let's face it, it is still risky, and the rewards just aren't that great.

A Lesson from The Big Short

There is a great movie called *The Big Short*. It is about the real-estate mortgage bond bubble that burst in late 2007. Investors lost

TRILLIONS of dollars when their mortgage bonds suddenly lost all their value. But, a few brave investors, who *un-balanced* their bets (I mean investments) realized HUGE returns, even though they risked almost nothing.

Now, this is not a lesson in bond investment. But, the book, *The Big Short*, inspired me when I learned that the best strategy might be to look at your risk/reward strategies in a totally different light. You don't want to try to get bigger rewards by taking more risk, and surprisingly, you probably do not want to LIMIT your reward potential by limiting your risk either.

It is this second strategy that I want to talk about here. It is a HUGE mistake, and it might cost you your financial future and freedom.

The Average Risk/Reward Balancing Act

You will hear me say this again and again. The majority of people try to minimize their risks by getting a job and working for someone else's dream. For example, if you manage a restaurant, you are taking minimal risk. You work long hours, but you do get a paycheck and you may even get a bonus. Your rewards might even be pretty good, but at what risk? You need to work more than forty hours per week as a restaurant manager, right? In fact, fifty or sixty hours per week is not uncommon. Now, you might make $120,000 per year, but at sixty hours per week, you are making about $40/hour. Not bad, but there is a LIMIT to what you can make, and in order to make that money, you CANNOT work fewer hours per week.

Look, this restaurant manager *thinks* he is maximizing his rewards. He is saying, "For someone like me, $40/hour is great money. I am doing very well."

It Is Better Than Being A Restaurant Owner

The manager might be thinking, "Well, I have no money invested in this business. On the other hand, the owner of the business has a HUGE investment in terms of money. He put in over $1 million to get this place started and running. And, if something goes wrong, he has to put in a lot more money just to keep it from closing. That is too much risk for me."

Yes, it is true, the owner does have a lot of money invested in the business. And yes, the owner could lose it all (and a lot more) if the restaurant goes bust. When we look at it that way, the manager does have a better, more balanced deal.

But, That's OLD Thinking, and It Is A Mistake

That restaurant manager (and almost everyone else who has a job) doesn't realize that they are investing (risking) a LOT of time and money in order to make ANYTHING on that job. And, they don't understand that their huge investment has a very limited return.

Think about this. In order to make any money on your job, you need to invest at least forty hours per week, every week, every year. You can't work less. If you do, your boss will fire you. Yes, you get vacation, but that is limited as well. How many companies give their employees more than 3 weeks per year of vacation? Not many! How many businesses give their employees more than 4 weeks of paid vacation each year? Almost none!

And, are you able to take your vacation when you want to take it? Can you just call in one day and say, "Well, I think I will take this next week off?"

Do you see what I am saying? You are making a HUGE investment (risk) just to get THE FIRST DOLLAR BACK! You are saying, "Well the owner of my company had to invest millions of dollars, just to make the first dollar in return." But, you might be doing the same thing.

"Wait", you are saying right now, "I didn't invest MILLIONS of dollars." No you didn't. But, on the other hand, you do not have millions of dollars, do you? And, it is extremely unlikely that you ever will! Why, because you are trying to balance risk and reward—big mistake.

Become Un-Balanced

Here is what you need to think about. You need to think of a strategy that minimizes risk—of all kinds, while completely taking the cap off the possible rewards! You need a strategy that does not put you into a silent trap just so you can earn the first dollar each year. You need to stop thinking of your job as a low risk operation. It has a HUGE risk—mainly because it takes up so much time—robbing you of control over your own life, while seriously limiting your rewards.

Think about that restaurant manager. Will she/he ever make more than $40/hour? Maybe a LITTLE more if she/he gets a bigger bonus, but what if she/he works all those hours and actually makes less the next year because the economy has gone down, or because the owner makes a big mistake and ruins the reputation of the restaurant, or even worse, hires his nephew to run the place?

Your Un-Balanced Future

Here is what you need to do. You need to find a company that has a great product or service, and also is LOOKING for people to help distribute that product/service. Find a company that requires a MINIMAL investment—less than $1,000. Get to work and get *trained* by that company at no additional cost. (Talk about a great investment! Even if you do not stay with that company, do you realize how powerful that training is? Man, you are getting un-balanced!)

Now, how many hours does that company require you to work each week, just to make the first dollar? NONE! In fact, they don't care how much work you do, or how little work you do. They are going to pay you for results. They don't care if you are dressed in a suit and tie at 6:00 a.m. They don't care if you want to take a vacation. They don't care (or even think about) your time. They are grateful for every, single sale you make. They have no minimums. They don't even have MAXIMUMS! They are so glad that you are working with them (not for them) that they will give you rewards for every, single thing you do for them.

And, if you do well, you will be rewarded far beyond the efforts you put in. You are un-balanced, and so are they. You see, by letting you work at your own pace, paying you only for results, they have a much smaller risk in you. They LOVE being un-balanced.

And What If You Build Business Builders?

Now, let's look at how to really un-balance the risk/reward paradigm. Yes, you can operate in an un-balanced way when you recruit customers for the company you work with. But, if you want to really go off the deep end—if you want to be truly un-balanced—think about recruiting other business builders. Yes, you have to make some investment of your time in doing the recruiting, but now you have established leveraged income. This means that the company will reward you, even if it isn't you that did the work to sell products! (Wow, you are really un-balanced now. Doesn't it feel great?)

Get Un-Balanced Fast

Don't wait. Start getting un-balanced right away. Learn the business and get to it. There is a whole world of un-balanced people out there, and they are waiting for you to join them. Aren't they worried that you will be competing against them? Not a bit. Why, because the rewards remain uncapped for un-balanced people.

That's why they are smiling. Wouldn't you like to smile as well?

MISTAKE

12

Seeing The Obstacles Instead Of Developing X-Ray Vision

Everyone has heard the old adage, "Focus on the reward, not the job," right? There is no doubt that is great advice. There is only one problem with that advice. It doesn't take into account that there is often something that is *hiding* the reward from sight. In other words, you can't even see the rewards, so how can you focus on them?

What is standing between you and your rewards? What is often directly in your line of sight? It is something BIG (at least in your mind). It is something that obscures your vision. It is something that is so scary, you can't seem to look away from it. It is so huge and seemingly insurmountable that you can't look around it.

In fact, the only way to focus on the rewards is to *look right through that obstacle (or fear, or challenge, or whatever it is) so that you can clearly see the rewards. For this, you need to develop* x-ray vision.

CAUTION: if you want to look *through* your challenges and see the solution, don't use an x-ray machine. X-ray machines are only good for looking *into* something, not through it. For example, when you go to the doctor and she uses an x-ray machine to examine you (to look for a broken bone, etc.) she is looking *into* your body. She isn't trying to look through it.

If you are at the airport, and airport security wants to examine the contents of your carry-on luggage, they don't want to see *through* the luggage, they want to look into it. That's what an x-ray machine does. And, you don't want to do that!

There Is Nothing Good *Inside* a Problem

Have you ever had a problem, and gone to an expert to get help? The expert will say something like, "Well, let's look into that problem." In the case of a malfunctioning computer, or a crime, looking into the problem might be a good idea. But, this is just technical stuff. It has nothing to do with the rewards. You simply want to *solve* the problem.

This isn't a bad idea. Solving problems is always good. Solving problems let's you move on in life.

But, we are talking about a higher level of motivation than simply solving a problem. We are talking about being able to see the REASON for solving the problem. That is a whole different animal!

You Need X-Ray Vision, Not an X-Ray Machine

What makes superman super? Is it because he can see into problems, or into suitcases or into bodies? No. That would make him pretty special, of course, but it isn't what makes him *superman*. He is so super because he can see *through* things. In other words, he can look past the big problem that is looming right in front of him, and see the possibilities that exist just on the other side of that problem. Now that is super!

This is what you want to do. You want to develop your own super power. You want to develop x-ray vision.

But Wait… Is There Really Any Such Thing as X-ray Vision?

Technically, no human can look through something. But, are you going to let your success get squashed on a technicality? I hope not. You see, true x-ray vision is only imaginary. After all, superman is just an imaginary character, right?

Okay, So Use Your Imagination

Your ability to use your imagination is going to separate you from the average person. The average person does not use imagination. The average person looks straight ahead, sees a big challenge or problem, and then collapses in frustration and fear. The average person might get as far as looking into a problem, but they cannot look through a problem, because they cannot imagine what is on the other side. They can only see what is in front of them, and that is why they get stuck.

What is imagination? It is the ability to visualize something that doesn't seem to exist right now. When you were a child, you were great at imagining things, weren't you? Did you have an imaginary friend? Did you imagine that you were able to fly, or to travel, or to do extraordinary things? As a child, you had a great gift. You could make things seem real—simply by using your imagination.

Well, as an adult, you still have those powers; you just don't use them. You are too afraid to imagine things. You have been taught, over the years, to "think practically." Everyone told you to grow up. This kills the ability to imagine things.

But that raw power is still down there, deep inside you. It still exists. You have the power to use x-ray vision. It isn't because x-ray vision actually exists. It is because your ability to imagine what is on the other side of a problem exists.

For example, if you wanted to lose some weight, you might run into some big problems. The problem might be that you don't have time to cook special meals. This problem looms in front of you, and it could very well derail your attempts to diet and lose weight.

But, you know *exactly* what is on the other side of that problem, don't you? It isn't even that difficult to imagine, right? You know that if you can overcome that obstacle, you will be thinner, healthier and less stressed out. You can visualize that, can't you?

Do You *SEE* What I am Talking About?

In the example above, I am not talking about how to solve the problem! I am not talking about looking into the problem and seeing what is really going on there (that would be like using an x-ray machine). I am talking about using your imagination (and therefore, your x-ray vision powers) to look right through the problem, and concentrate *solely* on the rewards.

Folks, this is a whole different way of thinking about your life, isn't it? You see, you have been taught to solve problems. You have been taught to use an x-ray machine to look into the problem, wallow around in it, spend time in it, and try to work out something that would help you resolve the problem. I am not talking about that at all. I am talking about looking right through the problem and spending ALL of your time on the rewards.

But, What About The Problem? Isn't It Still In The Way?

Absolutely it is. The problem is still there. You still need to find some way of getting around it, or solving it. But, now, you aren't looking at the problem, you are looking at the rewards!

Which is more motivating? Which is more likely to produce positive results? Which is most likely to separate you from the average people out there?

And, you know what I mean by the average people. They are the ones who only see the problem. They are the ones who *start* working on a problem, but when all they see is problems, they soon lose interest. You see, there are a lot of people on the *failure side of the problem*. They are the average ones. They got all the way up to the problem, and started working on it. They are the ones who are perplexed. They are frustrated. They are average.

But, there are a few people on the *success side of the problem*. These are the ones who saw the rewards, and then the problem didn't look so big. They are the ones who focused on the rewards, not the challenges. Not only did they use their imaginations to see the rewards, they saw the other people that had already overcome the problem and were enjoying the rewards.

And folks, when they saw *that* (the other, successful people who were already enjoying the rewards) they did it with their imaginations. They let their innocence overcome their skepticism. They built the rewards up in their imaginations, and then found imaginative solutions—not to solve the problem, but to join the successful people on the *success side of the problem*.

Pretty cool, isn't it?

Imagine that!

MISTAKE
13
Being The Prospector Instead Of Being The Gold

Okay, hang on. This is a HUGE mistake. I mean it's a BIG, BIG, BIG mistake!

How many people go through life, looking for something that will help them "strike it rich"? These people are like the old-time prospectors, wandering from place to place, dipping their gold pans into a promising creek, or digging tunnels into the side of a mountain. What are those prospectors looking for? They are looking for gold of course. Aren't we all?

Well, being a prospector is just about the worst thing you can do if you want to become successful. Think about it. How many stories have you heard about a prospector really "making it"? Let's look at a few examples right here in North America:

The Gold Rush of 1849

In 1848, James Marshall discovered gold in the creek behind Sutter's sawmill in California. It was completely unexpected. He hadn't set out to discover gold. But, the following year, *thousands* of gold-hunters showed up in California to stake their claims. How many of the estimated 300,000 "49ers" struck it rich? Not many at all, but the stories of the few who did captured the interest of *millions* of people. "Gold Fever" was rampant in the United States—and across the world.

The Klondike Gold Rush

A few decades later, more gold was discovered in the Yukon River in Canada's Klondike area. When word spread of the discovery in 1896, an estimated 100,000 prospectors went in search of their fortunes. According to Wikipedia, only about 30,000 of them actually reached the gold fields. (It was a dangerous and grueling journey to get from the coast to the actual gold mining area.) Only about 4,000 of the miners actually ended up making money from claiming gold from the frozen soil of the area.

You have to remember that travel to California and the Klondike was not easy in those days. In 1848, the population of California was not large. Most of the prospectors arrived there by ship or in wagon trains. Getting to the Yukon was even more difficult. Again, there was not much of a native population base there. Prospectors sailed from San Francisco, but also came from around the world.

Why were so many people willing to risk so much? Well… because it was for GOLD! As Wikipedia puts it:

"Gold rushes were typically marked by a general buoyant feeling of a 'free for all' in income mobility, in which any single individual might become abundantly wealthy almost instantly, as expressed in the California Dream."

Any Individual Might Become Instantly Wealthy

Prospectors flocked to a gold rush because any one of them could become rich—almost instantly. This means that anyone, no matter what their background is, could break free from the bonds that hold average people in place. A gold rush means possibilities. It means opportunities. The people who flock to a gold rush are dreamers— men and women with a vision.

Prospectors: Dream-Driven and Action-Oriented

Prospectors are unique individuals. They are risk takers. They *want* something more out of life. They are always on the hunt, and they are willing to do extraordinary things because they feel that the rewards are so high. They know that the odds are against them, but if they can just find the right stretch of river to pan, or dig down just a bit deeper, they might hit that Mother Lode that will make it all worth it.

Prospectors are always watching, listening and learning. They are actively seeking the next lead, the next possibility.

Prospectors "Easy to Find and Easy to Attract"

If you want to find prospectors, all you have to do is to look at places where gold is supposed to be found. That's easy. Everyone knows what the current "Gold Rush" is all about, right? Where is the Gold Rush today? It is in cyberspace. That is where everyone is looking for a fortune today. Many of the newest prospectors are working in cyberspace. They are in Social Media, Apps, Silicon Valley and other places. That is where the rush is now.

This doesn't mean that the actual GOLD is in cyberspace. It means that cyberspace is where prospectors are attracted. They are using cyberspace to keep up with trends and opportunities. The word is spreading—fast. When a discovery is made, information about it gets out immediately, and is spread from person to person, at the speed of light.

Contrast this with the California and Klondike Gold Rushes. Gold was discovered in California in 1848, but the first wave of prospectors did not get there until a year later. The first discovery along the Yukon River was made in 1896, but it wasn't until *2 years later* that the miners really began to show up.

And let me remind you folks, this is GOLD we are talking about. If it took almost two years for prospectors to react to the news out of the Klondike that there was gold to be had, imagine how long it would have taken to announce that farming was good up there!

Today, we get news instantaneously. It isn't just the first-person spread of news that is so quick. Second-hand news is just as fast. And, unlike the old days, that news does not get distorted in the second-hand stage, because it is written down, or has pictures, or videos that cover it. Today, we get first-hand accounts, but they are relayed by second, third and even tenth-hand prospectors.

What does this mean? It means that it might be far better to be the gold than to be the prospector. If you want to attract prospectors, that is easy. Just be the gold itself! If you want to attract them, be exactly what they are looking for. Let them find you in cyberspace, but be something solid and believable (the gold) so that they will be looking for you, and more importantly, RECOGNIZE you when they finally find you!

Did You Get That?

Folks, I hope you were paying attention in the last few paragraphs. This is a HUGE key to success—especially financial success. If you want to *attract prospects*, instead of being a prospector, you need to be EXACTLY what prospectors are looking for. You need to be the gold. You need to LOOK like gold. It must be completely unmistakable. There should be no doubt about it.

You see, while prospectors are all looking for gold, they are also all looking for it in the same places. That's what I mean when I say that it is easy to find prospectors. But, if they think you are another prospector, then they won't be as likely to stick with you when you find them.

Look, prospectors have something in mind. They aren't just hanging around, hoping that something is going to happen. They are actively seeking the gold. If they see it, and if they can believe it, they will stop their wandering and just hunker down to do some serious mining! Remember, great prospectors don't want to remain great prospectors. They want to stop being prospectors and start being rich miners.

Are You The Gold??

So, let me ask you. Are you the gold? Do you have something that prospectors want? Can you tell them about it, show them what it is, and have them believe you so they will stop looking and start digging in?

Do you know how to talk to prospectors? (Here is the first clue, don't talk like another prospector!) You aren't just trying to spread some news that prospectors would be interested in. You can START with that, but you have to quickly transition to being the gold: the thing they have been looking for all this time.

The Gold Brand

Folks, you have to brand yourself, and that brand has to be golden. It should take over everything you do. Your brand is that you are what the prospectors are looking for and now, they can stop looking and start enjoying. You see, you are a problem solver. You are a pain stopper. You are taking away their need to look, and replacing it with a desire to work—just so they can dig out the gold.

Get Ready to be the Mother Lode

In the mid 1970's, I lived in the Gold Rush area of California for a few years. What was I doing there? Well, I had just finished a year of service in a group called Volunteers In Service To America (V.I.S.T.A.). My college roommates were working in California, and I went to join them. Two of us ended up there in the Gold Rush country. (Yes, it is still called that, almost more than 150 years later.) The "Mother Lode" was supposed to be an almost inexhaustible source of gold. It was the dream of the prospectors to find that huge deposit of gold. I even had the pleasure, all those years later, of panning for gold in a stream myself. In fact, some of the people I worked with up there in the Sierra Nevada Mountains made some pretty good money in the summer, hunting under boulders for gold nuggets.

What did I learn? EVERYONE has that urge to strike it rich in a gold field. Not everyone does something about it, but the ones who do are easy to identify. They are looking. They aren't looking for other prospectors, they are looking—every day and in every way—for that gold!

Brand yourself as an opportunity, and prospectors will find you. Get the news out about your location by using the new telegraph wires: the Internet. That's where the prospectors are, and that's where you need to be with your opportunity.

Stop being a prospector and start being the gold!

MISTAKE

14

Being A Fear Leader Instead Of Becoming A Cheer Leader

It takes me a couple of hours to write each of these "mistakes." And, I have to tell you—I am really enjoying the time I am spending on this one! I have wanted to say this to people for quite some time.

Stop being a "Fear Leader" and start becoming a "Cheer Leader."

Who Are the Fear Leaders?

Fear Leaders are not just those negative, power-hungry people who think that their subordinates will respond only to the threat of losing something. (Although, these are certainly great examples of Fear Leaders.) Fear Leaders can be ordinary people as well. They could be the parent who tells her/his children, "If you aren't good, you are going to get coal in your stocking." (I am guilty of this one.) Or, it might be the boss who says, "If you don't get this work done, you are going to be fired." (Whoops, guilty again.) Finally, consider the teacher who tells a student, "If you don't start doing your work, you are going to flunk this course, and then you will end up working in a fast-food restaurant." (I don't think I ever said that to a student, but I certainly *wanted* to say it a few times.)

Folks, we are all Fear Leaders from time to time. And, in the case of safety or security, it certainly makes sense to use fear to change behavior. But let's face it, as a long-term tactic, this is really pretty dumb. After a while, fear loses its ability to create meaningful change.

And, it certainly is not a great motivator. But, the biggest problem with Fear Leading is not the damage to the person you are trying to frighten, it is the damage to YOU that has such dire consequences. (We will discuss this a little later in this section.)

Who Are Cheer Leaders?

Cheer Leaders on the other hand are all the teachers, parents, bosses, family members, friends, acquaintances, and team members who celebrate every victory—no matter who achieves it. Cheer Leaders do not discriminate. Cheer Leaders get excited for other people. Cheer Leaders know that accomplishing goals and objectives are often difficult. They "cheer" whenever they see someone overcome adversity—no matter how small it might seem.

My mother was a Cheer Leader. She got excited for *anyone* who succeeded at a task. I can still remember her as she let out her version of a cheer. She would lift up a knee, throw an arm into the air, and yell, "Hooray!" whenever someone succeeded.

In fact, at her funeral, we all did it in memory of her. It was a great moment then—and it was a great moment whenever she did it for all the people in her life.

Being a Cheer Leader is a great thing. It is beneficial for both the Cheer Leader and the person who is the recipient of the cheering. (Like the Fear Leader, I will discuss this more in this section.)

Important Note: I Am Saying "Cheer Leaders," not "Cheerleaders!"

Now, don't get confused here. I am not talking about cheerleaders. I have nothing against cheerleaders. In fact, I think they are terrific, and the things that *Cheer Leaders* do come directly from what *cheerleaders* have taught us. And, I have a personal link to cheerleaders. In high school, I was a cheerleader, and in college, I was the school mascot! My older daughter marched in the band for both high school and college—and they did lots of cheering. Finally, my younger daughter was a high school cheerleader.

But, for this section of the book, I am talking about being a *Leader* who *Cheers* for team members, subordinates, children, and well… for anyone who succeeds at something. Cheer Leaders help people to achieve their full potential by doing one, simple thing – being there to celebrate the occasion.

You see folks, Cheer Leaders make life better for all of us. Cheer Leaders are spontaneous. They show up unannounced, just at the right moment. They haven't practiced their cheers. They don't have a long routine. They just get excited whenever someone does well.

It is a different kind of leadership. It is leadership by celebration. And, it can be very powerful.

The Negatives (for the Leader) of Being A Fear Leader

Earlier, I promised to tell you why being a Fear Leader is bad for the Leader. Well, here it is: no one likes you! That's right, it *never* makes you popular. It *never* makes people want to be around you. It *never* attracts great people to your team. It isn't motivating to the person you are trying to use the fear on, but even worse, it is such a negative force that eventually, you lose perspective on what is really important.

Now, as I said, using Fear to scare someone into doing, or not doing something does work for some situations. And, it is even necessary in some cases. When we show teenagers one of those terrible accident videos in a high school driving class, it does have an impact. When we do warn an employee that they will indeed be fired if they don't make some changes NOW, it does (sometimes) have an impact. Sometimes, Fear is just what you need to instill in someone in order to get the desired outcomes.

But, let's face it. How does it make you look? More importantly, how does it make you feel? Would you want to be around you if all you heard was Fear? No, of course not.

I am a firm believer in the Law of Attractions. I want to attract the kind of people around me who would be nice to be around. I want positive people who work with me, or play with me because they like the way I make them feel. I know you are that kind of person as well.

So, stop trying to strike Fear into their hearts. Use Fear Leading ONLY in the extreme circumstances where it is truly needed.

The Benefits of Cheer Leading – For Everyone Involved

As I mentioned earlier, my mother was a fantastic Cheer Leader. Do you know what happened? As word got around that Kay Quain would get excited whenever you did something good, people started telling her when they did something good. My mom got good news all the time from people, and every time she heard good news, she gave out a cheer.

How about you? Would you like to be the one that people share their good news with? Would you like to be the kind of person who is attractive to people who are succeeding? Of course you would. You want to surround yourself with excited people. And, you want to be the reason they are so excited. If you believe in the Law of Attractions, then you want to be attractive to successful, happy people.

Don't Be A Fake

Now, let me give you a word of caution here. Don't get wildly excited about every bit of good news. Keep it in proportion!

It drives me crazy when I see the Little League Baseball banquets at the end of the season. ALL the kids get trophies. It isn't just the winners anymore. Kids get "participation" trophies. Everyone walks out of the banquet with hardware.

Now, I am not opposed to participation trophies. In fact, I think they are fun. I am a big believer in giving out cheers for people who are trying. But, I don't give out HUGE cheers for that kind of success (just trying). But, I also believe in the concept of winners and losers. I like competition. To me, it really sharpens people. It makes them hungry for more. It forces them to practice, and to work harder.

That's why I save my biggest cheers for the biggest wins. I want people to know that they have to do something to earn my bigger cheers.

To Be A *TRUE* Cheer Leader...

Now, I am going to let you in on a BIG secret that all great Cheer Leaders know. Sometimes you have to pull a reason to cheer out of the person you are cheering. Folks, this will really set you apart from the crowd. It is a VERY attractive quality, and it will attract the best kind of people to you.

Here is what happens: Someone does something good, and maybe gets an award. But, they are a little embarrassed about getting the recognition. They are afraid that it wasn't really that great. So, they play it down. They say, "Well, it really isn't much of a reason to get an award." The reason people act like this is because we are all taught from birth not to brag about our accomplishments. We are all taught to think of ourselves a "not really worthy of being singled out." (Well, I have to say that my mom never made us feel that way, but plenty of other people did.)

It is just part of the human condition, right? You know what I am talking about here.

So, what do the GREAT Cheer Leaders do? They start asking some questions about the accomplishment. They dig deeper. They actually *LEAD* the person you want to cheer into a sense of feeling even more proud of the accomplishment. Folks, that's Cheer Leading! That's the kind of thing that gets you into the Law of Attractions *Hall of Fame*.

Hip, Hip, Hooray for YOU

Look, I just know you are going to start being a better Cheer Leader, aren't you? After all, if you are still reading this section of the book, you have stuck with the Cheer Leading concept. You are a winner!

In fact, I am so excited for you that here is what I am doing. I am channeling Kay Quain right now. I am standing on one leg, with the other knee raised up. My arm is up in the air. I am yelling "Hooray for _____!" Now, just put your name in the space, and enjoy the fact that you are a winner.

Hip, Hip, Hooray!

MISTAKE
15

Living Invisibly Instead Of Positively Publishing Your Purpose

I believe in the Law of Attraction... well, I believe in PART of it. The Law of Attraction is basically a New Age restating of the old adage, "like attracts like." Basically, this means that *you attract the things you are thinking about.* According to the Law of Attraction, if you think negative thoughts, you will attract negative thoughts. If you are mean-spirited, you will attract mean-spirited people.

Now, like I said, I believe in this concept *in part.* Yes, negative people do attract negative people. Positive people do attract positive people. In other words, like DOES attract like.

However, the Law of Attraction (at least as it is defined in Wikipedia) says that thoughts are all part of a high level of energy. Furthermore, The Law of Attraction also says that *actions* are part of the same energy field. Therefore, thinking negatively will produce energy that will attract negative actions. My question is, "How far does that energy travel before it attracts similar energy?"

In other words, if I am sitting in my home in New Jersey, and I am thinking negative thoughts, how far away will the negative thinking and actions of others come from?

Do you see what I am saying here? I am just wondering how careful I have to be! And, on the *positive* side of things, how careless can I be and still get positive results? Does energy float around, looking for "like" energy, and then zoom in, in either a positive or negative force?

A Story of Two Hermits

There was once a hermit who lived in a cave, about four miles from the nearest town. Now, this was back in the days when hermits did hang out in caves, so we are talking about a long time ago—certainly before there was the Internet. It was definitely before the time when hermits had blogs and websites, and before they had hermit text messages that they sent to each other. Back in those days, a hermit was really a hermit!

This hermit (let's call him Herman) was a really miserable person. He complained all day long. He became a hermit because his complaining had driven off all his friends and family. He was so shunned by his society that he figured, "You know what? I might as well go off and live in a cave, because I don't talk to anyone anyway. At least in a cave I won't have to look at those people." I mean it, this was one *negative* hermit!

But you know what? No one noticed! He didn't attract any negative thoughts. He didn't attract any negative energy. He complained and complained all day long, and it didn't do a darn thing. He was just a hermit, and that was that.

On the other side of the woods, again about four miles from a town, there was another hermit. Let's call him Henry. Henry was a very positive hermit. Henry hadn't moved into his cave because he didn't like people. He moved there because he made a few bad investments and got into a really bad variable rate mortgage. Henry lost his home during a real estate slump. Henry moved into his cave because he thought, "Well, at least this way I have a really solid roof over my head." It all worked out.

Henry was a very happy hermit. Unlike Herman, he never complained. Henry didn't even complain about the mortgage broker who talked him into that sub-prime mortgage. (I mean... *everyone* was complaining about those people, but not Henry.)

But do you know what? Even though Henry was an extremely positive hermit, even though he had nothing but good thoughts all day, and even though he would break out in laughter for no apparent reason, no one noticed! No positive energy came flowing back into his cave. No one lined up outside his cave, waiting to hear some positive thoughts from Henry, in exchange for maybe a pie or something good to eat. Nobody noticed.

The Moral of the Two Hermits Story

There is no moral to this tale. It is just a story about two hermits. "But Bill," you might be saying right now, "How can there be no moral about this story? If there is no lesson to be learned from this, why did you put it into the book?"

Okay, there is a moral to this story, but I just wanted to drive you a little crazy so that you would focus on it when I told you. Is that mean of me? Perhaps a little, but didn't it get your attention?

And that is the moral of this story. I got your attention because you are reading my book! We have some *interacting with each other*. If I do something mean to you in one of my books, you are going to expend negative energy to get back at me, right? If you feel ripped off, you will tell other people not to buy my books. And, if you get a positive experience from reading my books, you will probably tell other people about it.

More importantly, if you make some meaningful and powerful *changes* in your life because you read something in one of my books, can you imagine the powerful ripple that sends out? For example, suppose you read one of my books and then you become more successful (not because of what I wrote, but because of what you did with the information you got from my book) and then your *children* learned some valuable lessons and THEY became more successful, wouldn't that be great?

Now, imagine if it spreads out to even more people. After all, tens of thousands of people are going to read this book alone. Not all of them are going to make significant changes in their lives, but what if even a hundred do? Will that change stop there? No, as they touch the lives of even more people, some of those people will make meaningful changes.

Now, contrast that with the impact (good or bad) that Herman and Henry the two hermits had. NOTHING. You can't contrast it because nobody was influenced at all by two hermits, no matter how disagreeable or agreeable either of them was.

Their energy didn't get around, did it? They kept it all to themselves.

That's Why I Am Not So Sure About the "Absolute" Impact of The Law of Attraction

Okay, now almost no one lives in a cave, miles from town, with no Internet. (I suspect there probably are some people who live in caves WITH Internet, but I'll bet the connections are very bad, and the download speed is terrible.) Today, we are all connected. Today, we all have the opportunity to send our positive or negative energy into the world, and get positive or negative energy (and actions) back.

But, we aren't all doing it equally! Some of us are trying to hide, just like the hermits, but perhaps with a few more comforts. Some of us are actually living invisibly. We don't put ourselves out there. We don't take advantage of things like social media, or email, or even something totally old-fashioned like the phone. (Do you remember when we actually spoke to each other?)

Now look, if you are *negative* and you are living invisibly, then I would like to personally thank you for staying out of the way. I mean it, thanks! But, if you are a positive person, if you have some good to offer the rest of us, if you could add to the world's joy in some way, or contribute to some good causes, then for goodness sakes, get out of your (virtual) cave and start sharing with us.

Why do we need you to do that? Because we can't start sending you positive energy back until you do! If we don't know what you stand for, and how you can help us, or how you can add to the world's delight, then how can we start being positive towards you?

Return to Sender, Address Unknown

Did you ever hear the Elvis Presley song "Return to Sender?" He sends a letter out to his girlfriend, and it comes back with the words "return to sender, address unknown." Okay, so in Elvis' song, the letter actually did reach his girlfriend, and she is the one who wrote "return to sender, address unknown" on the envelope, but let's not get too technical.

If the postman really *can't* find an address, the letter will come back with those words on it.

Folks, many of you are being sent positive energy, but we don't know your address, so the energy comes back to us. After a few attempts, we just stop sending it to you.

On the other hand, some of you have well-known addresses, but we don't know if you are a positive or negative person. In that case, no one is going to send you positive energy, because it is just as bad as having an unpublished address. You have an unpublished *purpose*! If you have an unpublished purpose, how do we know what kind of energy to send you?

Publish Your Purpose!

In today's world, where communication is instant, and where we can share information, feelings, intentions and rewards so easily, it is even more important than ever that you publish your purpose. What do I mean by "publishing your purpose?" I am talking about *branding* yourself with every thing you do, say and think.

If you want a positive brand, get out there and promote it. If you want people to believe in you, start acting like you are believable, and then brand it. If you want to give love, brand yourself as a loving person. If you want to attract possibility through business building and wealth creation, then brand yourself as that kind of person. If you want to make new friends, then be friendly and brand yourself that way.

And in all cases, please let us know how to send you the positive energy. If you want money, give us an address. If you want new friends, give us the address. If you are promoting a good cause, or a way of living that can help others and is a positive force, then give us the address.

Your brand is made up of your image and your actions. You then spread the word about those actions. You find other people who think like you do and you make sure that they know that you are the same kind of person.

Use your imagination. Be consistent. Keep at it. Be positive. And then…

Be sure to tell us how we can share the good stuff together.

Good People Are Looking For Good People

There is no doubt about it. Good people are looking for you. They want to find you, because good people want to put their positive actions and thoughts out there as well. They are positively looking for you—positively.

And I am positive you are going to like it!

MISTAKE
16

Selling Kindles Instead Of Building Channels

How did I come up with this mistake? Well, it's actually a story that involves an 84-year old man, a plane trip to Germany, a hard tile floor, and a dropped Kindle. How about a story that starts off like that!

Rocco and his Kindle

One of my great friends is Rocco. At the time of this incident, Rocco was 84. Rocco is one of those classic "learners" in life. He isn't *crazy* about technology, but he knows how to solve problems, and he isn't afraid to use technology to do it.

A few years ago, Rocco was flying from Miami, Florida, to Germany for a conference. Rocco loves to read on the plane, but it was going to be a long trip, and he knew that he would need more than one book. Rather than stuff heavy books into a briefcase, he decided to invest in a Kindle.

Rocco quickly learned how to load books on to his Kindle, and he put four really good ones onto the device in preparation for his trip. Off he went to Germany, Kindle in hand, and a very light briefcase in the overhead compartment.

I spoke to him after he got back from the trip, and asked him how he enjoyed the Kindle. "Well," he said. "It worked marvelously."

Rocco went on to tell me that he really loved the Kindle, because it was so light, and even in Germany, he could easily buy more books for it. But, there WAS a problem when he got home.

I prepared myself to listen to Rocco say something like, "When I got home, I really didn't want the Kindle anymore, so I just put it away, and probably won't use it again."

But, that wasn't the problem. It seems that Rocco was unpacking his bags after the long return trip, and he dropped the Kindle – on the hard tile floors that are so often found in South Florida. Apparently, the Kindle took quite a bounce, and when he turned it on, there was a big dark spot on two-thirds of the screen.

Rocco assumed that this product was a total loss, but he called Amazon anyway, just to see if they could do anything and hoping they would tell him how he could get it repaired.

After speaking with the customer service technician at Amazon for a few minutes, Rocco was shocked to learn what they were proposing. The Amazon rep told Rocco:

"Okay, we are going to send you a new Kindle overnight. We are also sending you a box to return your old Kindle. Just put it in the box, and we will pay for the shipping." And then, the Amazon guy spoke the magic words, "There is no charge. We will pay for everything."

Is Amazon Running a Charity?

Rocco was astonished to hear the news, but Rocco also has a great mind, and he was quick to point out something to the Amazon guy.

"Well, I don't want to be greedy" he said, "but I paid for four books. They are loaded on my *broken* Kindle. Is there any way you can replace them?"

At this point, you will not be surprised to learn that the good folks at Amazon looked up Rocco's account, and quickly loaded the four books on to his new Kindle. The next day, Rocco got his brand new tablet, along with his books, and put the old Kindle into the pre-paid mailer to send it back.

Amazon Is Not Selling Kindles

Amazon is not in the business of selling Kindles because there isn't any profit in it. I just went to Google and looked up Kindle prices. The most expensive one that I saw in my admittedly quick search was just under $80. I also saw used Kindles selling for a lot less, and what looked like some new Kindles for about fifty dollars. I don't know if these prices are representative of what Kindles sell for these days, but it is what I saw.

Let me ask you, how much money could Amazon make by selling those machines for $80? How much money could they make if they had to compete with other tablets?

Think about it: Amazon has sold MILLIONS of Kindles, right? How much would it cost them to set up a Kindle maintenance center to handle all the potential complaints, repairs, warranty work, etc. It would be a nightmare.

It isn't the business that Amazon is in! Amazon is in the business of selling books, not Kindles. Sure, they sell all kinds of stuff, but they REALLY like selling digital books. So, they practically give their Kindle away, and if there is a problem, they simply give the customer a second one—with only a few questions asked. It is a lot cheaper than trying to work with all those customers who dropped their Kindles on a tile floor.

Keep It Simple and Keep the Cash Flowing

I will say it again: Amazon is not selling Kindles; they are selling books. And, they sell books to people who have *working* Kindles, not to people who have broken Kindles. Amazon makes a lot more money by selling a $10 book than they do when they sell Kindles.

You see, no one buys more than one Kindle at a time. But, *everyone* buys more than one book at a time (or at least, they buy a lot of books over time). And Amazon likes to sell books to people who buy books.

"So," You Might Be Saying, "How Does This Apply To Me?"

Amazon knows that their customers will only *stay* their customers if they can buy books in an easy and convenient fashion.

So Amazon sets up channels. They would rather sell digital books that have absolutely no maintenance costs, no printing costs, no inventory, no shipping, no customer complaints about the books being broken or lost and no real overhead. Amazon DOES pay a royalty when someone buys the book. Amazon pays the royalty to the author. But, and here is a big but... *when* does Amazon pay the royalty to the author? They pay the author ONLY after a book is sold and the money received.

That's a Great Business!

Yes, it is a great business. And, while Amazon has you in their store, they hope to sell you other things as well. In fact, they even put advertisements right on the "buy" page when you are choosing a book. The text says, "People who liked this book also liked..."

And, once you are a Kindle buyer, Amazon has your credit card information on file. Now, the next time you make a purchase, Amazon doesn't even have to ask you for a card. It just gets easier and easier, and you buy more and more—and they never have to hassle with Kindle repairs and problems.

Build a Channel

Folks, be like Amazon. Build a business where people who are ALREADY buying things, a lot of things, will buy them through you! Develop a business that gives people what they are already asking for. Take a little bit off each piece you sell, and let someone else worry about the delivery, the accounting, the marketing, etc. This is called "setting up a channel."

When You Set Up The Channel, You Own The Channel

There are HUNDREDS of THOUSANDS of companies always looking for new ways to get their products into the hands of the customers. These companies already do all the manufacturing, legal and accounting work, shipping, and advertising. In return, they are looking for people who will get their product into the hands of customers who are product loyal. These customers recognize ease and convenience and will buy more and more of the product.

And, that's what you want as well. You want to find a company, link them with customers, and then take a little piece of every transaction. This is building a channel.

It Costs Almost Nothing to Build Channels

If you are merely representing products, and not manufacturing them, it costs almost nothing to build a channel. In fact, with the Internet today, it is almost FREE!

And, no one will make you buy a storefront. You can set up your channel in the minds of your customers. Match products and ideas with what these people already want, and with what they are already buying, and you have a perfect match. You are now selling books instead of Kindles.

You Will Love It

It's a great story – the story about how you became successful after realizing that you were making this mistake. If you like romance, it has romance. If you like adventure, you will see adventure. It is funny and sad at the same time, but always, in the last chapter, there is a happy ending.

And, if you do it right, you won't have to wait until the end of the book for the happiness. It will have a happy beginning too.

MISTAKE
17
Eating Your Steak Instead Of Feeding Your Cash Cow

Don't get excited. I have nothing against eating meat. Indeed, I have nothing against eating a nice, juicy steak. I love those nice steak restaurants, with lots of wood and low lights. They are great for business dinners, for romantic evenings with my wife, and for a celebration when one of my books is published.

But I know one thing: eating steak costs money. It isn't cheap. I only spend money on steak when I have the money to spend. Before I eat steak, I make sure I help to grow my cash cow!

What is a Cash Cow?

I went to Google (of course) and asked the question, "What is a Cash Cow?" I got the following results:

cash cow: Well-established brand, business unit, product, or service that generates a large, regular, predictable, and positive cash flow.

Just look at that definition. I see words like "well-established brand" and "predictable and positive cash flow."

I like that idea!

You need a positive and predictable cash flow, don't you? You need some kind of business that gives you POSITIVE cash flow. You see folks, a J-O-B does not give you a predictable and dependable positive cash flow. It might APPEAR that it does, and I am not suggesting that you should not have a job. I am just saying that your job is not dependable any more. It is not predictable.

But, being *unpredictable* is not the big problem with a J-O-B. Your job is not a Cash Cow for another, very different reason. This reason that your job is not a Cash Cow is not based on uncertainty. Your job is not a Cash Cow because it is not Positive Cash Flow.

Let me explain.

You see, according to the definition above (and every other definition of Cash Cow that I could find), a Cash Cow is only a Cash Cow if it gives you back more than you invest in it. Your J-O-B is a break-even proposition at best, and a cash-sucking, time-losing, money pit in many cases.

On your job, you go to work and trade your time for dollars. How much do they give you per hour for every hour that you work? They give you EXACTLY what they think your time is worth. So, if your time is worth $25/hour, you will get paid $25/hour, right? I mean, if your time was worth more, wouldn't they pay you more? If your time were worth less, then they would surely pay you less, so your time must be worth exactly what they are paying you. It is simple math.

Your Forty-Hour Week

If your time is worth $25/hour, and you work 40 hours in a week, you are going to get paid $1,000 for your work.) This is simple math. You simply multiply $25 times 40, and you get $1,000.

How much did you invest in that week's work? You invested $1,000 of your time, right? (Yes, you did. You sold your time—you and your boss agree.) In fact, you invested 40 hours of your time that week. That is an investment of $1,000 from you, and you got the same amount back.

Oh no, wait a minute… you DID NOT get $1,000 back, did you? No, you paid taxes on that money. The government kept some of that money, right? Will you get that money back later, with interest? No. Well then, who does get your money? Some of it goes to great services, like the road system, schools, etc. Some of it goes to some not-so-great services. You don't know what those not-so-great services are exactly, you just know that some of it goes to it because it isn't going to you and you can't even imagine where it is going!

Some of your hard-earned money goes to people who are in need. You don't have a problem with that, right? I mean, people sometimes need help. In the United States, we have programs to help people who really need it. It is the right thing to do, but it does diminish your return on your invested time value.

On the other hand, some of your hard-earned money goes to people who just plain do not deserve it. Some of your money goes to prisons or to people who just won't work, or people who make really bad decisions in life.

I Am Not Against Taxes and Helping People

Please don't get me wrong. I am not against taxes and helping people, or building roads, or supporting education, or health care, etc. I understand we need these things. I am simply pointing out that some people, when they read the definition of a Cash Cow, will say, "Well, my job and my paycheck are predictable. I can depend on them. I know I will get paid every week. Therefore, my job must be a Cash Cow." I just want to point out that a Cash Cow actually *generates* a positive Cash Flow, and your job does not. Your job is definitely NOT a Cash Cow. In fact, it isn't even a good investment when you start to see that you are trading a valuable asset—your time—for a paycheck that is actually worth less than the money you put into this thing.

So, What Is A Cash Cow?

First of all, a Cash Cow is a business. It produces money from your investment, and the money it produces will exceed the investment. The money from a Cash Cow keeps coming in, month after month, year after year. It is dependable. You can expect to get that money every month, or week, or whatever.

How Do I Feed a Cash Cow?

All businesses require some kind of continuing input of time or money. Remember, the idea is to GROW your Cash Cow continually, because things change and you need to be an active participant in your business so that it will continue to grow. Some customers will die, or stop using your product, or simply lose interest. Some of your key people or associates will move on, for whatever reason. For these reasons, you need to do *something* to keep your Cash Cow fed.

But, smart Cash Cow raisers find a way to *leverage* their investments of time and money so that the Cash Cow will put out a positive Cash Flow. And, if you feed your Cash Cow correctly, you don't have to do much at all after a time of building.

The Cash Cow Mindset

If you are serious about setting up a Cash Cow business, you need to find a product or service that is in high demand. By this I mean that a lot of people want it, and they want it all the time! For example, if you sell large appliances, it is extremely difficult to set up a Cash Cow business. Why? Aren't large appliances in huge demand, by a lot of people? Yes, they are, but only every 10 to 15 years or so!

Large appliances are out as a Cash Cow for another reason. You need a tremendous amount of money in inventory, and in a storefront in order to sell refrigerators. That is a very expensive proposition. So, in order for your Cash Cow to give off a positive cash flow, you need to sell a LOT of refrigerators each month. And guess what? You need to sell the same number each month thereafter, just to pay the overhead.

You must do thousands of dollars in business before you see a dime in positive Cash Flow.

Just To Be Sure, Let's Make Sure You Know what Positive Cash Flow Is

What is positive Cash Flow? It is when the money you lay out each month is less than the money you get back in your pocket. If you have a business, and your overhead each month is $5,000, then you need $5,000 in profits (not sales, profits) in order to break even. However, if your overhead is just $1,000 each month, and you have $5,000 in profit, your CASH FLOW is positive. In fact, I am positive it is $4,000/month!

That's a positive Cash Flow. That's why we tell you that your job is not producing a positive Cash Flow. If you work 40 hours per week, and your time is worth $25/hour, your overhead is $1,000—and that's just in the amount of time you invested. Don't forget, you still need to buy clothes, have a car to get to work, etc. When the government takes money out of your paycheck, and you pay for the time you invest, and you pay for all the gas and insurance you need for your car, and the clothes you must buy, well… you can quickly see that this is no positive Cash Flow, and no Cash Cow.

If My Job Can Never Be A Cash Cow, Then What Do I Do?

You need a business of your own, and you need to make sure your overhead in that business is as low as possible. Don't get bogged down in a business with a big building, lots of employees, minimum payments or sales each month, etc. These are all Cash Cow killers. (You don't want to be accused of killing those poor old cash cows, do you?)

In today's world, there are thousands of businesses that have almost no overhead. They require very little investment in terms of either time or money. When your overhead is so low, it is easier to feed your Cash Cow. It is therefore easier to develop a positive Cash Flow.

More importantly, look for a business that allows you to <u>leverage</u> your time and effort. Look for a business that attracts other people to partner with you. Soon, as you help them grow their businesses, you will start to get a piece of the cash flow they generate. This is how you feed a Cash Cow.

But What About The Steak?

In the beginning of this chapter, we said the mistake was "Eating Your Steak Instead of Feeding Your Cash Cow." What happened to the steak part?

When you eat steak and do not have a positive Cash Flow, you are adding to your overhead. We established that steak is expensive. It costs you money to eat steak. While you are growing your Cash Cow, try to do everything in the world to decrease your monthly expenses. Then, take that money and feed it to your Cash Cow! And we aren't just talking *steak* here. Stop consuming all those expensive things that make your overhead so high. For example, do you really need a $400/month car payment for that luxury gas-guzzler? Is it possible, while you are feeding your Cash Cow, to drive a more modest car?

Robert Kiosaki talks about this in his fabulous book *Rich Dad, Poor Dad*. He describes what people do with a raise when they get it. For example, if someone gets a $6,000/year raise, that is an extra $500/month in income. (Wait a minute, it isn't worth $500/month, because you have to pay taxes out of that.) But nonetheless, when most people get a raise, they buy things like a new car. But, they don't buy it outright, after all they only got a $500/month raise. They might be buying a new car for $40,000, but they use the $500/month to pay the monthly payments, right? Now, they are trapped. They have to keep on working so that they can pay off that new car. They just raised their monthly overhead by quite a bit. And, if they are like most people, they are going to buy another new car before that one is paid off. That's what I mean by steak. It is a luxury item that adds to your overhead.

When Do I Get To Eat Steak?

Grow your Cash Cow first, and then use the positive Cash Flow to buy your steak (or whatever you want to buy). Once you are Cash Flow positive, you can decide what you want to do with the money. It is just a matter of priority.

Always remember this, "The steak always tastes better when the cow pays for it." Now that's a great line!

MISTAKE

18

Trying For Timing Instead Of Filling The Funnel

As I sit here writing this, it is March 17, 2016. For all of those people out there who are not of Irish descent, I probably need to tell you that it is St. Patrick's Day. St. Patrick is the patron saint of Ireland, and all over the world, Irish folk, and those who just like to celebrate like the Irish, are all wearing green, and ready to go out and hear some great music, and if you are very lucky, catch a St. Patrick's Day parade. In cities like New York, Boston, and San Francisco in the U.S. there are great times to be had. But, nothing is like St. Patrick's Day in Ireland. I must be one of the luckiest people on earth, because right now, I am sitting on the balcony of our rented apartment, overlooking the bay in Galway, Ireland.

In a few minutes, my family and I are going to walk down the street, about ten minutes away, and be right at the very start of the St. Patrick's Day parade in Galway. (Galway is Ireland's original capital, and the center of the study of Irish culture.)

Are we here by accident? Did we just happen to "hit it at the right time?" No, we planned to be here. We made reservations almost a year in advance. We purchased our plane tickets, rented the apartment, and arrived in Ireland a week early. We traveled throughout the rest of the country, but we arrived here last night, and we are all ready to enjoy the celebration at the heart of Irish culture.

Our timing is perfect—but only because we worked on it for a year.

Now, timing is much easier when you do not have a moving target. But, that isn't the case with most things in life. If you are trying to sell something, build enthusiasm for an idea, communicate effectively or get people to make a decision, timing is very difficult. In fact, it is downright mysterious.

Is The Target Really "In The Mind?"

Most people think of money as "being in a bank," but that isn't the case. Today, money is really all in the mind. And, those minds are not naturally disposed to giving that money away. So, you need to go to the minds of other people in order to get the money you want from them. And, those minds are moving! They are moving both in terms of actual physical locations, and in terns of openness to your idea or product.

In order to get those people to open their minds in order to buy (or even listen) you have to be there, in the right place, at exactly the right time. This is why we call it a moving target.

Mining the Mind

If you want to get something from someone else, or if you want them to even *consider* something you are trying to convey to them, you are up against a whole host of obstacles. (That's why so few people actually succeed at success.) Most people just don't take the time to set things up so they can succeed.

However, if you are reading this book all the way to this Mistake Chapter, you are doubtless VERY interested in getting other people to do something. Am I right? You want something more out of life, and to do it, you must get the cooperation of others.

The 5 Steps In Buying

No matter what you are doing to succeed, it involves someone else buying something—perhaps a product or idea. Either way, the process is the same. They have to go through the five steps in order to make a buying decision. Otherwise, they are not going to buy from you. Instead, they are going to buy from someone else.

What Are The 5 Steps In The Buying Process?

1. **Problem Recognition** – No one takes any action until they realize they have a problem. In fact, they won't even *listen*.

2. **Information Search** – Once someone realizes that they have a problem, *then and only then* will they start looking for information on how to solve that problem.

3. **Alternative Evaluation** – Once a potential buyer has assembled some information about alternative choices for solving the problem, *then and only then* will they start evaluating the choices. You see, most people just don't jump on the first alternative they come across. They want to make sure that the idea or product they are going to buy is the best one (the most price-effective) for solving their problem.

4. **Purchase Decision** – once someone has recognized they have a problem, found information about solutions to that problem, gone through a number of alternatives to determine which one represents the best value, *then and only then* they MIGHT make a purchase. But, they might not. They might decide that the problem isn't as costly as the solution. (I'm telling you, it is tough out there!)

5. **Post-Purchase Anxiety** – Now, here is the really crazy part, and it is where a whole lot of people fail. You see, even after the average person recognizes the problem, searched for information, compared alternatives and made the decision to buy, they are STILL not sure if they did the right thing. In fact, at this stage, post-purchase evaluation, a lot of people return the product, turn away from the idea, or stop making the changes that they committed to just a few hours or days ago. AND, more bad news, the

post-purchase evaluation process portion of the five-step buying process could last forever!

Like I said, "Timing Is All In *Their* Mind."

Look at those 5 steps. Can you see how difficult it is to get the timing right? First of all, nothing even begins until the prospect is firmly in step 1: Problem Recognition. If they aren't there, nothing else matters. So, how can you time your approach to be there, just at the right time, and in just the right place? How can you hit that moving target at just the right moment, with just the right message?

The Funnel – Timing Problems Solved

If you are trying to sell people on an idea, or trying to get them to buy a product from you, or to build a business with you, you can't depend on your ability to meet them at exactly the right time, every time. In order to increase your chances of success, you need to build (or join) a system. This system is called a "Funnel" because it is wider at the top, and narrower at the bottom. You want hundreds of prospects to enter the funnel, and you are savvy enough to realize that most of them are going to *leave* the funnel during one of the stages. In fact, you are going to realize that many of them will leave your funnel in stage 5 Post-Purchase Evaluation, even after they made a purchase or commitment to you.

However, when you set up a funnel, you are also going to realize something else. If the funnel is a good one, there will always be more people in the funnel. More people will be at the top, and more people will be at the bottom. And, this means more success for you!

BE WARNED: This isn't some kind of "hands-free" system. You still have to *work* your funnel, and you still need to have human contact. But, when you have a funnel, it is easier to know when people are in the different steps of the Buying Process.

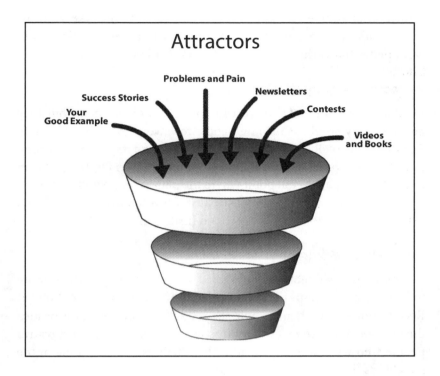

Look at the top of the funnel. There a number of "Attractor" examples: videos, blogs, networking, and positive social media posts.

All of these things are attractors, but the real secret is to have attractors with a trigger. For example, when you post online videos, ask for comments or "likes." Collect friends, contacts, email addresses, etc.

When people begin to notice that you have changed your personal habits—such as getting work done on time, dressing better, listening more—you want to have some sort of mechanism to make sure that they have some way of moving into the next level of your funnel. Use business cards, and get them to watch, listen or meet with other attractors in your funnel. Add them to a list and keep in contact with more positive messages. Folks, building attractors at the top of your funnel is so simple and easy. Just get started. It will take you just minutes a day to begin building your funnel's attractors. Some will work better than others. Some won't work at all. Stay with it.

Attractors – They Work

Attractors can build interest in your ideas or products, but they are especially good for helping people to have problem recognition. Remember, we call it "Problem Recognition" for a reason. Sometimes, people have a problem, but they are not aware of it. Or, the problem has not yet made it to the point where the pain is so great that they are ready to go to the next step. Stir the pain with your attractors, and then always give your prospects a way to go further into your funnel.

Keep Them Moving

As soon as someone has triggered your interest, give them more ways to move through the funnel. Share information (After Problem Recognition) or let them sample the rewards of your business or idea during the Alternative Evaluation stage. Get them around positive people who will support your idea. Let them experience some of the benefits as they weigh all the alternatives.

And finally, keep them involved and positive. If you set up your funnel correctly, they won't pop out the bottom as soon as they make the purchase or decision. Keep them in the funnel, and keep them supported and happy.

And, That's Why We Do It!

You see folks, if you have satisfied customers/business associates, you are really solving your timing problems. Now you have dozens, maybe even hundreds or thousands of ambassadors out there—all with the ability to reach new prospects at exactly the right time. That's the really big advantage of building a funnel. Make yourself timeless and put the work into filling your funnel.

By The Way...

After writing the first few paragraphs of this mistake chapter, I went to the parade with my family in Galway, Ireland. It was fantastic. I never did get back to the process of writing this chapter for the rest of the day. Instead, I am finishing it on the plane ride home to New Jersey. Isn't that great timing?

By the way,

MISTAKE

19

Losing Late Instead Of Learning Early

Two men were sitting in a sports bar, watching the Tour de France bicycle race. The Tour de France is a grueling, three-week-long, 2,200-mile trek through some of Europe's highest mountain ranges. The racers descend into valleys and through the rough cobblestone streets of many towns. They race in all kinds of weather, from bone-chilling rain to searing summer heat.

The first man said, "I don't understand why those racers would put themselves through such hardship. It certainly seems like a lot of work and pain."

"Well," said the second man. "The winner can make millions of dollars in endorsements and prize money. That person is famous throughout the world of cycling. It is a great honor to win the Tour de France."

"Oh, I can understand why the winner would want to do it," said the first gentleman. "But why would all those other people put themselves through the effort?"

Wouldn't it be great if we knew what the outcome of a race would be before it even started? It would save most of us a lot of trouble. If you knew you weren't going to win a race, would you go through all the trouble of participating in it? Would you say to yourself, "Maybe I will try something else. After all, if I am not going to win this race, I can surely find something else to do that will be a better use of my time."

Folks, most of us are running a race that we can never win. Unfortunately, we spent a lot of our lives running that race anyway. Isn't it time for us to learn our lessons early, instead of waiting until the end to discover that we lost?

Playing The Game

In my book, *Overcoming Time Poverty*, I talk about three kinds of games that we humans play in our lives. They are the sports game, the corporate game, and (for some of us) the leverage game. Let me recap how these games work, in order to show you the dangers of losing late instead of learning early.

The sports game: in every country and culture on earth, professional sports players can earn huge amounts of money. We love our sports. In the United States, we encourage our children to participate in sports. Some of our children will excel, and others won't. Very few will go on to become professional. They give up so many things in their lives in order to excel. They practice all the time. They travel. Many of them give up their leisure time in order to pursue their sport. And, as they reach higher and higher levels of proficiency, the top competition for those few professional spots gets tougher. Almost none of the men and women who have aspirations to play a professional sport will ever reach that level of play. And, even if they do, very few of them will make the kind of money that will make the effort worthwhile. But, each year, as new generations pick up a basketball or football, new dreams are born.

On the other hand, if you are not going to make it to the ranks of the professional athletes, there is some good news. Generally speaking, you will know if you have the right stuff by the time you are in your early 20s. Let's face it, if you haven't reached the professional level by the time you are 25, it should be abundantly clear that you are never going to make it. For some people, this seems like a bad outcome. "Imagine," they say, "You are only 25 years old, but everything you want in life is suddenly out of your reach. All your dreams are dashed."

I look at it differently. Wouldn't it be great to know for certain that your plan isn't working by the time you are 25? If you know you have to come up with another plan, isn't it great that you still have the rest of your life ahead of you? At 25, you have plenty of time to make the changes necessary in order to achieve personal and financial success. At age 25, most people are not yet burdened by a huge mortgage, children, and the other trappings that we pick up along the way.

The corporate game: the second most common game that people play is the corporate game. In many ways, it is like the sports game. People enter the corporate game with great expectations. They believe that if they work hard, they can achieve great wealth and success in the corporate game. Like professional athletes, they spent a lot of time preparing for the corporate game. They go to school and study for years. They take entry-level jobs, just to get into the corporate game. They trade thousands of hours of their time, and delay their gratification for other things, just to climb the corporate ladder rung by rung.

And, just like the sports game, fewer and fewer people reach the higher levels. As they go up the ladder, the competition gets more and more fierce. In order to keep on progressing, players in the corporate game need to spend more and more hours each day at work. They give up their leisure time. They postpone things that would otherwise make them very happy.

But, the corporate game has one distinct disadvantage. By the time you figure out that the corporate game is not going to give you what you want in life, it is much later! You might be in your 50s or 60s by the time you figure it out. And, when you do, there might be precious little time left in life to adjust. What if you spend hours and hours of your life, working in the corporate game, just to get laid off because the economy goes bad? What if that happens later in your life? Will you have the resources in order to adapt and change? Or, would you spend your remaining years struggling and trying to find the financial resources that will allow you to enjoy your remaining time? Yes, the corporate game can be rewarding—but it is certainly not rewarding for everyone. And often, by the time you make that discovery, it is far too late.

It isn't your fault. You did all the right things. But, for a variety of reasons (the industry becomes obsolete, technology replaces workers, or perhaps a recession) you are without a job. Suddenly, you are in your 50's or 60's and you are no longer needed. You spent a lifetime doing one thing, and now that thing is gone.

But It Doesn't Have To Be That Drastic

Of course, there are a lot of other ways to lose at the corporate game. Perhaps you make some bad investments with your savings. Or perhaps you suddenly realize that spending 50 hours a week for 50 years just isn't going to give you what you want. At the end of all that time, what do you have? How much is left after you pay for your home and your new cars, your kids' college tuitions, some unexpected medical bills, and all the other things that cost you so much money? At the end of 50 years of hard work, do you have all the money you need to retire—for the next 30 years? Or, will you be living on that dreaded "fixed income"? Will you be forced to scrimp and save every day—watching every penny—just so you will have enough for the basics in life? You see, you don't need to get laid off or fired in order to have lost the corporate game. You can go through a whole lifetime of better than average earnings, only to find out that your dreams of living in a warm place, playing golf or fishing, are still out of your reach.

If You Lose Late, You Are Not Alone

You may find some comfort in the fact that the vast majority of people lose late. They spend their whole lives doing something, because they believe it is all going to work out well. But they don't understand that the world has changed. You can work 40 or 50 years of your life and still live another 30. You can spend hours and hours each week, working at a job, and never really get to enjoy all the things that life has to offer. You can give up 50 weeks a year, just so that you can have two weeks off. This goes on for years and years. It is "what everyone is doing." And so, you do it as well.

Ironically, the same people who lose late at the corporate game will teach their children the perils of the sports game. They will say to their children, "Don't think that you are going to be successful as a professional athlete. The chances of you succeeding at that are very, very slim. Yes it's great to enjoy the game. It's great to have exercise and relaxation. And, it is even okay to try for the big prize in sports— to compete at the professional level. But don't forget to get a good education. When sports don't work out, you will need that education to get a good job. You need to have something to fall back on. Play sports, but go to school at the same time. Be ready for when you need to make the switch."

You have heard people say that, haven't you? You probably even said it yourself. Everyone knows that you need a "Plan B" if you are thinking about playing the sports game. But, the same people that spend so much of their time telling their children not to depend on the sports game for financial success spend their whole lives playing the corporate game. And after 40 or 50 years, they are in the same position as someone who failed at the sports game. The big difference is that they didn't have a "Plan B."

How To Learn Early

It doesn't matter which game you play, you can still learn early. All you need to do is to look around you. Look at the people who have been doing what you are doing. Look at the people who have been doing it for 20 or 30 years more than you have been doing it. How are they making out? What do their lives look like? Do they have time and money? Are they relaxed? Do they get to take vacations with their family? Are they stress-free? These are valuable questions to ask yourself.

Look folks, it is fairly simple. Most people never really succeed in life. Oh, they work hard and get along. They keep their jobs and make a pretty good living. They have a decent home and a couple of automobiles. They take their two weeks of vacation a year. They sacrifice in order to put their children through college. Most of them are happy. Most them are thinking to themselves, "Well, I'm doing as well as most of my friends." But is all the effort worth it? Are any them breaking free of the bonds that hold average people captive, in a state of stress as they worry about money day by day? Are they financially independent? Do they have what it takes to weather the storm if economic times turn bad? What if an unexpected event, such as an illness befalls them? Do they have the financial time and emotional resources available to them?

I am not saying that this is a crisis. I'm not saying that you spend every day of your life afraid. I'm not saying that the majority of people are desperate and unhappy with their lives. I'm just saying they could do better. In my mind, working for 40 or 50 years, just to worry about every single dollar every single day is certainly not winning. Maybe in your mind it isn't a big loss, but you certainly can't think that that is a win.

Let's go back to those men who are riding their bicycles through the Alps and the Pyrenees in the Tour de France. For the winners, it was all worth it. But how do the losers feel? When they began the race, were they hoping for a better finish?

Folks, all I am saying is that you need a plan B. If you can look around you and say to yourself, "You know, I think if I'm going to go through all this trouble, working for 40 or 50 years of my life, maybe at a job I don't even like that much, I want to win." Then you need a plan B. You have to have something else to do. If everyone you see around you is ending up in a place where you don't necessarily want to be, it is time to change the route of your life. And, by simply observing other people, you can do it early. You don't have to wait until it's nearly over to discover that you did not win. That's all I am saying. Don't panic—just get realistic.

And, it is far better to do it early.

The Leverage Game – Your Plan B

In other parts of this book, I talk extensively about how to leverage your equity. Leveraging your equity means that you create assets that help produce a steady, dependable income for you. I'm not going to spend a lot of time going over it again here, because you will get it in other chapters in this book. And, if you have been one of my readers over the years, you know that I talk about it in my other books as well. Leverage your time. Build assets. Let your assets work for you. That is your plan B.

However, since this is a chapter on "Losing late instead of learning early" I'm going to spend a little time talking about your plan B—especially in terms of when you should start implementing it.

Almost all of my readers are playing the corporate game. You all went to school, and you have all been working hard at a job. You are doing the right thing, right? Go back to the introduction of this book. Read again where I talk about the problem with making mistakes. The big problem isn't that you are making mistakes; it is that you are making mistakes while you think you're doing the right thing. Anyone who makes mistakes while they think they are doing the right thing is someone who is going to lose late in life.

Now, the great thing about having the leverage game as your plan B is that you don't have to wait until you have lost the corporate game in order to start winning at the leveraging game. You can do it while you're in the middle of the corporate game. You could do it while you're still playing the sports game! You can start the leverage game at any point in your life. Even if you are towards the end of your time in the corporate game—in your 50s and 60s,—It is not too late to begin the leverage game. The leverage game does not require the investment of large sums of money. The only thing you have to do in order to start playing the leverage game is to start playing the leverage game. Look around you. Don't look for the people who are just like you. Don't look for the people who are working 40 or 50 years of their life just so they can end up living on a fixed income. Look for people who learned early. Look for people who are playing a different game.

How can you find them? How can you find the people that will help you start your plan B? Start listening to opportunities. When someone says to you, "I came across something pretty good. Would you like to take a look at it with me?" Don't hesitate. It never hurts to look. Be open. Be willing. And be in a hurry. Remember, not only do you want to learn early, you want to learn as early as possible. Get busy!

How late is it? None of us knows how late it is in our lives!

That's a little scary, isn't it? Don't wait. It is never too late until the day it is too late. If you didn't learn early, then at least learned today.

MISTAKE

20

Making A New Year's Resolution Instead Of Making A Last Year Resolution

Let's pretend it is December 31st. You are about to end a year of your life. A new year is about to begin. What are you thinking? What will you (and millions of other people) do as the New Year dawns?

You make resolutions. You look back over the past year and say, "I want this year to be different. I am going to…"

1. Lose weight

2. Make more money

3. Build better relationships with my family

4. Learn to _____

5. Etc.

We are always looking ahead when we make these resolutions. We have a world full of good intentions. We might even join a support group, or download an app to help us keep our promises to ourselves.

And then…

Studies show that we tend to break our New Year's resolutions about the middle of February. That's right. The average is just six weeks. All of our good intentions are gone: all of our plans and promises. Gone. We go back to doing the same things we always did.

Why Does This Happen?

I have a theory about why this happens. You see, we are looking at a *lifetime* of change. We make a new year's resolution, and say to ourselves, "From now on—from this day forward—I am going to start/stop/change/complete/etc. some thing, some activity or habit. You can fill in the blanks here. You have done it, right? You have made the pledge that from now on, for the rest of your life, things will be different.

Folks, I think that scares people half to death. After all, if a habit or practice is so bad that it would figure prominently in your very first day of the New Year, with the anticipation that it will not happen again for the rest of your life, it must be a pretty big deal! I mean… what kind of thing makes it on to your New Year's resolution list? It isn't something like, "I will try to put more ice in my lemonade glass, starting right now, and continuing for the rest of my life. My lemonade habits will be completely different from now on, and it is going to improve my life. When I become a new person through putting more ice in my lemonade, people will respect me, dogs will love me, and women/men will swoon over me whenever I walk into a room."

No, the New Year's resolutions are saved for big things. They tower over your imagination, and haunt your dreams. When you finally do give up your resolution, on or before February 15, you feel terrible. It makes you feel so bad because you didn't even make it to March.

I'll bet there are plenty of people who don't even get out of January.

You see, if this thing is so big that it will get on your New Year's resolution list, you have been wallowing around in that bad habit for a long time. If you decide that your New Year's resolution is to lose weight, you can bet you are struggling with that fact. You hate the weight and want to definitely get rid of some of it so that you look better, feel better and can find clothes to wear.

So, when that extra dark chocolate cake comes your way, down the long dinner table, on January 1 at your first dinner of the New Year, imagine how you are struggling? Imagine the temptation, the split-second decision, and then WHAM! Your resolution is over.

How about your resolution to spend more time with your family this year? It is going so well, but then, WHAM! There is a football game on, and it is the college championship game. You can't miss that. Your friends are counting on you to come over and watch that "BIG GAME" with them. Just like that, it is over.

Finally, suppose you resolved to work on a new business this year? You make a list of contacts. Actually, you did just fine with the list building last year. It was the NEXT STEP you have problems with. You are having terrible difficulty making contacts, or setting appointments. You had resolved that you would not be afraid this year. It was going to be a new year, and a new you. But then, you are so afraid, and now you are so guilty!

Folks, the feeling of looking ahead for the rest of your life, and not giving yourself the time to change a lifetime habit, or fear, or lack of motivation, is just too much. It is too much for almost anyone. It certainly has been too much for you, right?

Give Yourself a Year

That's why I suggest that you make a last year resolution. With a Last Year resolution, you aren't suddenly faced with a "yes or no" deadline on January 1st. Instead, you will have a full year to make the changes.

In a Last Year resolution, you say things like, "This is the last year I will spend at my current position at work, or in my business."

Or, you might say, "This is the last year I am going to spend at this weight. I will never again start a new year at this weight."

Or, "This is the last year I am going to have credit card debt that I can't pay off."

Can you see the difference? You are cutting yourself a break. You are giving yourself some room here.

Are you likely to break your resolve by Feb. 15th when you make a last year resolution? Of course not. It is only February 15th. The year is only six weeks old. You can still make progress towards your goal—whatever it is.

It Is All About Making Progress

You see, when you make a Last Year goal, you need to set some small goals along the way. If you miss one, you can still do better next month. You can still work on your goals, right?

But, when you set a New Year's resolution goal, we tend to make it an all or nothing proposition. We say, "I will never" or "I will always…"

Setting a Last Year resolution is so much easier. And guess what? Making small steps towards a goal is much more sustainable. It is so much more realistic.

When you make small steps, and don't expect perfection, you are much more likely to hit your targets. But here is the thing, even if you miss your total goal, the process of working towards the goal, and taking SOME steps, is much better than doing nothing.

And, taking small steps forward is so much easier than becoming perfect all at once.

What are your Last Year goals?

Why not make a list of your goals for the Last Year resolution right now? Why not?

"But wait Bill," you might be saying, "It is July 1, not January 1. How can I do it now?"

That's the beauty of a Last Year resolution. You are merely saying that this is the last year you will find yourself in your current position. Saying it is the "last year" for something can mean two different things.

1. You might mean that you will have made the change by December 31st of this year—the last day of the calendar year, or

2. You might mean that you are going to give yourself until next July 1 to make the changes.

In either case, all you need to do is to set some interim goals, start working on it, and NOT worry about it when you fall short, or have a setback.

That's it. It will set you free, and make your next February 15th a lot better, with less stress and less guilt.

Happy Last Year!

SUMMARY
A Final Note From Bill Quain

Folks, it was a real pleasure to write this book for you. I know it will help you. Just take your time, and read some of these mistake chapters again and again. Talk about them with your friends. Share them with some of your business associates. Most importantly, discuss them with your family and closest advisors. Each of these mistakes will mean something different to every one of my readers. You might not "get it" with some of the mistakes, but others will really hit you hard.

I have already heard from some of my advance-copy readers that they have "favorites." It all depends on what is going on in your life right now. And that is why it is so important to share these ideas. You never know who will need one of these mistake chapters right now. You can change lives. I know you can, by sharing this book. And, if you share it with the right people, at just the right time, you might just change your own life (and fortunes!) as well.

I can tell you that *writing* this book had a great impact on me. In the Introduction section of the book, I told you the story about the investor who lent $50 million to a start-up company's executives… TWICE! While that one episode in my life led me to understand that we are all making some crazy, success-crushing mistakes, it also led me to the realization that we didn't know we were making them. As I began to put together a list of mistakes we are making, it occurred to me that most of us (including me) actually thought we were doing the right things all along. And, if we just did MORE of the things we were already doing, we would finally overcome the boundaries that surround average men and women, and achieve real, lasting success.

But remember the title of this book; "You Will Never Get It Right By Doing It Wrong." That makes sense, doesn't it? No matter how many times you do something the wrong way—especially if you don't know you are doing it the wrong way— you are never going to succeed in this life.

Let Me Hear From You

Let's stay in touch. I would love to share some more thoughts on the mistakes that we make, and I would love to hear from you about which mistake was your favorite one. Why not check out my website at *www.quain.com* to share your ideas, and to get some free, 60-second videos you can share with your friends and business associates.

Remember, my favorite mistake chapter is "Living Invisibly Instead of Positively Publishing Your Purpose."

Let's Positively Promote Our Purposes – together.

With great thanks to all of my readers,

Bill Quain

ABOUT THE AUTHOR

Bill Quain, Ph.D. is the author of 20+ books on personal growth, wealth creation and personal business ownership. Many of his books are international bestsellers. His books are published in more than a dozen languages, and have sold over 3 million copies worldwide.

Bill knows the meaning of overcoming adversity. He began to lose his eyesight at age 14. Today, he is legally blind and walks with the aid of a white cane. Despite this handicap, he is still writing, teaching, speaking and traveling the world. He delivers his messages of hope and inspiration to audiences of all sizes.

People who like this book will also like these other books by Bill Quain:

10 Rules to Break & 10 Rules to Make

Overcoming Time Poverty

Happy Leap Year

Money Talks... *finally!*